Ring of Fire

This book is dedicated to
Act for America
Corona, California Chapter
and their members and friends.

The National
Act for America Organization
had aroused the passion and spirit within me
to understand the wiles of the
enemy we face in America.

A special thanks
To the Core Freedom Team members.

And last but not least, my
wife, children and grandchildren that
they may enjoy the same freedom and liberty
I have enjoyed for over 70 years.

Ring of Fire

This novel is a work of fiction.
Some of the plots and story lines are
taken from local newspapers and
articles which includes references to
people, events, establishments,
organizations or locals and are intended
only to provide a sense of authenticity
and are used fictionously.
All other names, characters, and places are a
product of the authors imagination or if real,
are used fictitiously to enhance the
story lines of the events that take place.

Southern Life Media
P. O. Box 631, Corona, California 92878

Copyright 2015
R. L. Longworth

ISBN: 13:978-1518712234
ISBN: 10:1518712231

Printed in USA

Ring of Fire

The Revolution:

The battle cry in 1776 by Patrick Henry, still rings volumes to patriots today, "Is life so dear, or peace so sweet, as to be purchased at the price of chains and slavery? Forbid it, Almighty God! I know not what course others may take, but as for me, give me liberty, or give me death!"

Watching a 4th of July parade, the seven year old looked up at his daddy and asked, *"daddy, daddy when did America fail?"*

His father, stunned by the question, stared in space and shrugged his shoulders. *"It's partly my fault."*

"Daddy those soldiers are wearing a different uniform and what are they shouting?" he asked.

Dad lowered his head and turned the other way.

Preface

The story you are about to read is fiction.

However, there are many facts, figures and substance in this book that are relevant for today.

One, I am a retired minister (50 years) preaching the Gospel of Jesus Christ, with a vast knowledge and understanding of the Word of God. God gives us insight and signs that relate to the last days as described by Daniel, the Apostle Paul and John in Revelation.

I have also been involved for six years as a CORE member of a local chapter of Act for America, a grass roots originazition that promotes National Security and the awareness of political Islam in America that relates to our freedom and liberty under the Constitution.

I am also a student of political science and history as it relates to America and our founding fathers addressing our Republic, the Declaration of Independence and our Constitution.

There is no doubt in my mind regarding the veracity of events described in this novel — many of which are fictitious in nature — yet drives the point home. We are in a battle for the very life of our freedom and liberty.

> There are over 35 Homegrown Terrorist Camps, plus other terrorist and sleeper cells in America.

> Islam is not only a religion, it is just one of the components that make up Islam. Islam's ideology is one of military, political, social, jihad and finally religion.

> Are all Muslims terrorist? NO!

> Are all terrorist Muslims? YES!

Let me state first of all, I am not against Muslims and their worship of Allah but I am against Islam's ideology and Sharia Law. Sharia Law is not compatible with our Constitution and has no place in our court systems. I advocate for American Laws for America Courts through out our country.

Prologue

As the Roman Empire fell in the last
100 years of their civilization, could
America follow suit and become
the modern Romans of the
21st Century

"Ho, Ho." they laughed at the warning of Seneca.
"Rome fall? Never."

To Roman citizens living in the glitter of empire—enjoying an explosive frenzy of building, with huge cities, bejeweled with rising marble columns, with paved, pleasant tree-lined avenues and rushing through triumphal arches of yet additional conquests; hearing of the exploits of this or that great general —- Rome was impregnable.

She was the world — and the world was Rome.

To speculate for one brief moment that all this could soon collapse — that the ravages of wars, taxation, mounting debt, crime, race riots, subversion from within, political assassinations, natural disasters and public apathy would one day bring Rome to utter collapse and ruin, was not only unimaginable to them — it was folly to the heights of idiocy.

And to millions of American and even the British people today, the thought that America and Britain could suffer a similar fate — though with more modern consequences — seems equally ludicrous.

But Rome fell!

The year 2014

Today the United Kingdom (England) is on the verge of falling under the domination of Islam as the British parliament and the high courts are giving way to more and more Muslim demands. As Rome fell, even so will the United Kingdom unless the tide of 'political correctness' is forfeited and the Brits take back their country.

Rome fell!

Now the voices of the ancient scoffers are as still as the silent war and the rubble of ancient Rome — mute testimony to a once proud empire.

Unable to stem a tidal wave of violence, wild spending, wars, degenerating morals of an unbelieving public, willing to accept the society of their day — they were led to the final fate they all denied was possible. Millions of ancients lived to see the impossible happen.

Rome fell.

And there were causes for that huge empire's drift into chaos and final collapse—specific, definable reasons.

Is America doomed to the same watery grave that possessed the heart, soul and spirit of Rome.

Today, millions the world over stand in open-mouthed awe of the achievements of space-age man, laser rays, heart transplants, computers, cell phones — the dazzling advances of technology serve to convince millions that we have become scientifically secure, impervious, eternal.

This supreme confidence in man's own abilities is evidenced all around us. But fortunately these are only a modern form of idolatry, and salvation from growing world troubles by the vehicle of science will prove as empty a dream as Roman prayers to Jupiter, Venus or the Emperor.

As Rome fell, we too can fall.

The major causes facing America today:

1. The breakdown of the family and the rapid increase of divorce.

2. The spiraling rise of taxes and extravagant spending — (debt ceiling.)

3. The mounting craze for pleasure and the brutalization of sports.

4. The mounting product of armaments (under this administration we are reducing our military might) to fight ever-increasing threats of enemy attacks.

5. The decay of religion into myriad and confusing forms, leaving the people without a uniform guide.

Everyone of these factors is brimful and running over today. You read it in your daily newspaper, watch it on television, your cell phone or the internet — growing incidence of divorce, broken homes and juvenile delinquency, inflation and taxation, the pleasure binge, the revelation of the gigantic Obamacare debacle, immigration, jihadist and the Muslim Brotherhood and the influx of Islam on American values.

A high school history teacher in Moreno Valley, California list several things that will destroy a civilization. He tells his students about the rise and fall of great civilizations (such as the Roman Empire).

1. First, history shows that no nation can survive the tensions caused by having two or more competing languages and cultures. So we should turn America into a bilingual country.

2. Second, let's invent "multiculturalism' and encourage immigrants to maintain their culture while we promote the idea that all cultures are equal.

3. Third, let's make sure we celebrate diversity rather than unity. We must replace "melting pot" with "salad bowl". Let's have all cultural sub-groups enforce their differences rather than emphasize similarities.

4. Fourth, let's continue to make our fastest growing demographic group the least educated by continuing to allow Mexico to export its poverty to the United States.

5. Fifth, we must establish the culture of "victimlogy." Let's get all minorities to think that their lack of success is the fault of the majority.

And finally, we must use terms like "racist" and "bigot" and "xenophobe" to describe people who oppose the culture of diversity or the doctrine of victimlogy.

Can this American disaster be stopped in time?

Perhaps the Brigade gathered around the Ring of Fire will be able to slow or stop the bleeding and give America time to adjust and fight the malady that faces us.

Will the Brigade patriots rescue America in time or will she falter like the great Titanic and be swallowed in a frigid cold watery grave.

Time is not on our side.

We must make quality decisions that will effect our country from this point forward—a decision to surrender or fight for the freedom and liberty delivered to us by our forefathers.

Freedom is not free. It cost—check history and count the cost in lives, property, possessions and let's not make the same mistake by not learning from history.

Edmund Burke quote:

"The only thing necessary for the triumph of evil is for good men to do nothing."

Ring of Fire
The Revolution
2014 and beyond

Ex-Marine Colonel A. J. Jackson warmed his hands as the blaze of the fire floated upward toward the stars. He coughed and cleared his throat. "Men, welcome to The Brigade, the Ring of Fire. We are on a mission, as the enemy has declared Stealth Jihad on our country."

"Sir, can you explain Stealth Jihad?" The young man from the mountains of Appalachia asked.

"Soldier, the enemy knows they can not compete with our military power, so they are using our Constitutional rights to under mind our foundation and destroy us from within," He told him.

"Do you mean our first amendment rights, sir?" He asked.

"Absolutely! They are using the guise of religion, our rights to worship. Most people call this, the separation of Church and State." said the Colonel. "The Constitution by our founding fathers did not say this," as he pulled a small book on the Constitution from his jacket and read the first and second amendments."

"Our mission consists of fighting fire with fire. We will turn their tricks on them. While they are fighting in the courts of public opinion, leading our legislators around by the nose, preaching Islam is a religion of peace, we will find their leaders and hunt them down like mad dogs."

Standing in the shadows near a large oak tree was the silhouette of a man. His gaze was like a poker, that had been left in the fire so long, the tip was 'white hot.' He stepped from the shadows and introduced himself.

"Patriots, I am retired Army General Lee."

Several of the men jumped back a few steps. Fear gripped them; as they viewed this giant of a man.

"The President and his administration have fired or demoted over 200 commissioned officers in the past two years, depleting our military of brilliant minds that have hundreds of years of experience," he told them.

"Is a revolution in the future? Yes!"

It is now time to fight back . . . taking our country back to its original foundation," he barked loudly. Colonel Jackson handpicked you for this mission. You will be trained as sniper/assassins. I already understand that many of you rednecks are sharp shooters. We need you to sharpen your wits. Under the cover of darkness we will succeed. We already have a brigade of volunteers from the State of Tennessee, while others are forming in Alabama, Texas and other parts of the South. Soon we will have brigades in all of our Appalachian states, even some outside of our region.

Turning toward Colonel Jackson, the General said, "the Colonel will fill you in on camp protocol, code and password. You will return to your homes and jobs during the week, but two weekends a month will be mine. Is that clear?"

"Yes sir" as the sound echoed through the trees and bounced off the mountain.

"I didn't hear you. Is that clear?" he shouted.

"Yes sir!"

"Colonel take charge of your Brigade."

Colonel Jackson made his way to the front. He stood still for several minutes before he addressed the men, "You are taking an oath of secrecy. You will not under any circumstances reveal our mission, code or password," he instructed them. "Your family will be inquisitive, but understand, mum is the word."

"Is there any questions?" he asked.

"Great. I want you to pair up by twos. Each one will be responsible for the other. I want you to know one another inside and out. You will become one identity. You will be known by your code name only. If there is ever a problem with law enforcement, you will not reveal any information about the Brigade, its mission or code of honor."

The ten hand picked sharp shooters were paired off. Some walked toward the wooded area while others mingled around the fire.

Ben England, looking around, noticed a tall thin man warming his hands by the fire. He had not been paired with any of the others, so Ben took a few steps forward, introduced himself.

"I'm Ben England. I live close to a small town on the Kentucky, Tennessee border."

"Glad to meet you Ben. I'm Joe Capps. I live in a rural area in Claiborne County."

Joe Capps and Ben England hit it off from the very beginning. Smiling, Joe told Ben he was a winner of the annual firearms shoot-out in Claiborne County.

"I could shoot the apple seeds out of an apple hanging about 30 feet in the air and not even damage the fruit," Joe said.

"Man, that's some pretty decent shooting," Ben said. "Reminds me of the time I went squirrel hunting. Ole Blue had this squirrel treed. The squirrel was jumping from limb to limb and Blue was howling for all he was worth. I estimated the next jump, of that squirrel flying through the air, bang, right clean through the head. The squirrel did a triple tumble flip, fell at Blue's feet."

Both men slapped each other on the shoulder, laughing. They walked back toward the ring of fire and joined the others. As the men set around the ring, Colonel Jackson rose to his feet.

"Patriots, I have some information for you to memorize before you return and then it must be destroyed. Also you will find an outline and bio of some of the greatest leaders Appalachian has ever produced. Men like General George Patton, Pvt. Audie Murphy and Sgt. Alvin York. Let the heroics of these leaders be your guide as we accomplish our mission. Our next meeting will be two weeks from tonight. You are dismissed."

The men jumped to their feet. Snapped to attenttion. Colonel Jackson, turning around, walked away from the campfire. The men, looking at one another in a quizzical gaze, picked up their gear and dispersed from the camp site.

Ben walked through the woods to a clearing of small bushes and the path that led to the backyard of his wood frame home. He whistled for Ole Blue. The dog jumped the fence and made a leap into his arms. He knelt down, rolled Blue over and over in the grass. Walking up the path, Blue continued yipping at his feet. Ben bent down, patted him on the head, before he stepped on the wood porch. He opened the screen door, and walked in the kitchen, smelling the aroma of coffee. It wet his appetite. After pouring a cup, he picked up two pieces of bacon, chewing on them while walking to the bedroom. Cracking the door, he saw Sarah was fast asleep. Walking back toward the kitchen, he stopped and peeped in the kids room. Sonny and Bonnie, his six year old twins were asleep.

Sitting at the kitchen table, Ben turned his head, looking at the clock on the wall, he muttered, "wow, it is late and six o'clock will come way too soon to suit me." Ben rose from the table, picking up two more pieces of bacon, and placed them in a biscuit, then downed the rest of the coffee before heading to the bathroom to prepare for bed.

In the bedroom, Ben slides under the covers, and gently placed his hand on Sarah's hip. Sarah turned over and gave him a soft kiss, then turned over and pulled the covers up around her shoulders.

The sun, shining through the bedroom window, broke the darkness of night. Sarah Lynn rose from the bed, made her way to the bathroom to freshen up.

In the kitchen, she reached in the cupboard for the coffee can, a cherished gift from her mother. She remembered the many times her mother used it to keep the grounds flesh. She pulled off the Saran Wrap, picking up a scoop of coffee and placed it in the filter. While the coffee was brewing, she walked to the bedroom, shook Ben several times. "Ben it's almost six. Breakfast will be ready in a few minutes. When you get up, go and wake the kids. They need to get ready for school."

Walking back into the kitchen, Sarah opened the back door, threw Blue a cold biscuit and a piece of left over bacon. Closing the door, she made her way to the refrigerator. Opening the door, Sarah reached in for the sausage roll and eggs.

From the kitchen she hollered for Ben to get up …. get the kids up. They can't be late for the school bus, as she placed several pieces of sausage in the iron skillet.

"Ben England. I said to get up now. Take care of the twins while I finish fixing breakfast," she yelled. "I have a big day planned at church today, so toast it is. I have a special women's luncheon tomorrow and I want everything to be perfect."

As she finished cooking breakfast, she whispered a short prayer, "Oh Lord, can't you do something with Ben.

He is a good husband, a good provider and he works hard."

"Who are you talking to Lynn?" asked Ben, pulling the chair out from the kitchen table.

"Oh someone you don't know. I was just muttering out loud how good a husband and provider you are."

"Ok, Ok. So you have been talking to that preacher again. Who knows, it took my dad over forty years to come to terms with God, so keep praying for me."

Running through the house Bonnie cried, "Sonny won't let me use my hair brush. Make him give it to me," she bellowed.

"Sonny James England you give her the brush," Sarah hollered. "Hurry up and I'll fix you breakfast. Do you want toast and eggs?"

"I don't like eggs and toast," he screamed from the bedroom. "I want cereal."

Lynn placed two bowls at opposite ends of the table. In the red one she put a small amount of cereal and milk. The blue one was filled nearly to the top with the same.

"Breakfast is ready. Hurry up or you will miss the school bus," she told them. Sonny and Bonnie bounced around the corner and sat down at the table. In a few minutes the bowls were empty and then they were off to brush their teeth. Sonny pushed Bonnie to one side, rushing from the bathroom to the kitchen, to pick up his sack lunch and books. Sonny bolted out the door, hollering bye Mom, bye Daddy. . . hurry Bonnie."

Crying, Bonnie walked slowly to the kitchen, put her small arms around her mother's waist. Sarah patted her on the head and softly spoke, "we'll get even with Sonny. You can have the TV the first hour," kissing her and ushered her out the door.

Lynn returned to the kitchen, bending over she kissed Ben on the head. "They are a hand full, but I love them," she said. She poured herself a cup of coffee and sat down in the chair left vacant by Bonnie.

"You came home quite late last night. What was so important to keep you out so late?" she asked.

"Honey I really don't like keeping secrets from you, but this is one that I must. All I can say, he paused, it is important to our family and the security of our country."

"OK for now, Ben England," Lynn told him.

"Thanks for understanding. I must get to work. I'll see you shortly after five. I love you Sarah Lynn." He opened the door and kissed her bye.

"Whew, guess I will sit a spell. May as well have another cup of coffee," she muttered.

Chapter 2

At lunch time, Ben pulled the papers from his lunch bucket. The front cover did not give him a clue what was inside. It simply read, What do these people have in common? He opened the paper. His eyes glanced at the picture. I know that man he thought to himself. Now, what does he have in common with all these folks. Ben leafed through the papers. There were pictures of *Pvt. Audie Murphy, Sgt. Alvin York, Pat Tillman, John Wayne*, several Presidents and a host of others. He looked at the back page. These important people all came from Appalachia. Ben turned to the third page and glanced at the figure, which jumped off the page, a picture of General Patton.

He paused for a moment, flashback of the movie *Patton* with *George C. Scott* swept over his mind. He set up straight in the chair, before turning back to the first page.

The first page introduced the readers to a part of American history. It showed that Appalachia had at least a dozen Presidents beginning with *Andrew Jackson* , *Chester A. Arthur, Ulysses S. Grant, Theodore Roosevelt* (through his mother), *Woodrow Wilson, Ronald Reagan* (through his mother) and *William Clinton.*

Their unique soldierly traditions formed the

backbone of the country's military, particularly in the Army and Marine Corp.

Ben swelled with pride, as he read of such great men like *Stonewall Jackson, George S. Patton and Ulysses S. Grant*. He read about *Sgt. Alvin York,* the hero of World War I and *Pvt. Audie Murphy* the most decorated soldier of World War II.

The papers continued to tell the story of the fiercely independent individualist people known as the Scots-Irish. It goes against their grain to think collectively.

As America rushes forward to another redefining of itself, a spirit of defeat, political correctness and the end of our freedom and liberty by a class that pushes us into the abyss, these proud patriots and or their descendents will rise to the task that is before them.

The Appalachians are the molten core, at the very center of its unbridled, raw rebellious spirit that helped build this nation from the bottom up. They face the world on our feet and not on our knees as weaklings. They were born fighting. And if the cause is right, they will never retreat.

You have been selected as a special breed to fight for our Constitution and its guarantee of freedom and liberty. This message will not self destruct, but should be read from time to time as a reminder that we are at war. If these rednecks or rebels could accomplish so much with limited weapons, just imagine what we can do today.

Ben finished his lunch, placed the paper back in

the lunch bucket.

On the way back to work he had a sparkle in his eyes. "I'm so glad to be counted a part of this brigade, fighting for my wife and children that they may continue to live in the land of freedom and liberty."

Two weeks later:

Ben kissed Sarah Lynn and the twins, before he opened the kitchen door, and stepped off the wood porch. Ole Blue barked a few times and nipped at his feet. He padded the dog on the head, turning to wave at his family.

Running double time up the path and out of sight, Ben's huge frame melted in with the brush and trees. In the mountains he felt the sense of nature and the security of his surroundings. His mind wandered to the times, as a young boy, his dad had taken him squirrel hunting.

Ben stopped at a large boulder, looking closely he could see the etching of his initials BE and an arrow running through the letters. He paused, looking up at the sky and softly spoke, "Thank you dad for the memories."

Hearing a rustle in the bushes, Ben knelt down beside the boulder, lifting his rifle to his shoulder. Ben's eyes, keen and sharp, focused on the direction of the sound.

Silence.

He muttered, "Could it have been a deer or small animal. Why didn't it move or make another sound?"

Suddenly, a voice behind him, "lay your rifle on the ground, do not turn around and spread eagle."

Visibly shaken, Ben laid spread eagle on the ground for several minutes, listening for any movement.

Silence.

He raised his head, slowly turning to see who was behind him. Realizing he was alone, he jumped to his feet and dusted the dirt and leaves off his fatigues. Reaching down, he picked up his rifle, and cautiously moved through the woods until he arrived at the sentry point leading to the camp. Two soldiers stepped from the woods, prompting Ben for the code. Ben whispered the code and continued walking the short distance to the ring of fire, meeting up with the other party members.

"What took you so long?" asked Captain Owens.

"Sir I don't know what to make of it. I was kneeling at a boulder when I heard sounds. I stationed myself in a defensive mode and listened for the sound again. All of a sudden, a voice from behind me . . . ordering me to lay down my weapon. Several minutes of silence. Slowly I turned my head and no one was there.

Some of the men broke out in laughter.

"Guess there was a ghost or a spook," one stated.

"Hey man, it's not funny," Ben said.

"What did the voice sound like—boooooo," laughed another.

Captain Owens stopped the hazing.

"Ben this was a teachable moment for you. If you

are to be a good sniper and a member of the Brigade, you have to be alert and know your surroundings at all times," he told him. "Besides it has happened to most of us at one time or another."

"Thank you sir. I will be more careful from now on," Ben said.

Alright men, load up; ammo, water and some beef jerky. We will be gone until dark. In the open space just over the mountain, you will find targets of various sizes and shapes have been set up. I need to see who is the sharpest "hawk eye" in the Brigade."

Chapter 3

"Colonel Jackson will be here briefly. We will start our training for the next couple days. It will be intense. Whatever you brought from home has to be discarded. This includes any food or water. We're going to learn to live off the land and find our own drinking water," Captain Owens told them.

Grumbles came from some of the men, discarding the goodies. They turned their canteens and water containers upside down, pouring the precious substance on the ground.

"First of all, we will do some stretches. This will limber your muscles and warm your ligaments. Then we will do the hard work out. You will need to follow me. Do you understand?"

"Yes sir," came the chorus.

"Run in place. Hit the ground. Run in place. Hit the ground. Run in place," he bellowed. "Double time up the hill, now."

Ben and the others were huffing and puffing when they reached the top of the hill. Ben bent over touching his knees with his hands, cried, "oh for a drop of water," he muttered.

"There's a creek with fresh water about 1000 yards to the east of here. The first man to reach it, gets the first drink," Captain Owens told them.

Rising to a standing position, several men took off running to be first to drink from the creek. Ben was in the middle of the pack; running, catching his breath, he muttered, "this is not like squirrel hunting. This is torture."

Colonel Jackson standing in the shadows, took notes of each man at the water hole. Watching each man drink, splash their face, neck and hair with the cool water.

It was tri-light when the brigade moved double time back to camp. Several men were bent over, touching their knees and breathing hard. There were quickly called to attention, when Colonel Jackson stood before them. Men I want to commend you for a fine workout on your first day. "I would like to call out the following members of this Brigade for their unselfish act at the creek. Many of you were ready to take a bath or even a swim if the water were deep enough. Men, this is survival. You must learn discipline, for it may someday save your life. Suppose the enemy were waiting at that water hole or even an animal. Some of you would be dead or seriously injured."

Captain Owens saluted the Colonel. "Chow time will be at eight thirty tonight and wakeup call will be at five. Find a rock or a soft spot on the ground for sleeping. Good night," Captain Owens said, walking out of their sight.

Ben, looking at his partner, Joe Capps, laughed out loud. "And to think we volunteered for this crap. If we survive this training and don't die first, we just might make good snipers." Joe shook his head in agreement.

"Every muscle in my body is hurting. I need to go back to work Monday just to rest up," Ben laughed.

Joe laughed. "Me too buddy. Let's see what's for chow?"

The grub wasn't what you call from 'mom's famous kitchen;' a pan of beans, beef jerky and a piece of bread. Ben looked at the small amount of food on his plate. "Boy, I can't wait to get home to Sarah Lynn's cookin'."

Taking a field jacket out of his back pack, Ben folded it and placed it next to a small tree limb on the ground. Joe folded a small blanket, placed it on the ground. Both men yawned. "Time to turn the lights out," Joe said.

Ben responded, "My lights are already out."

Chapter 4

Upset that Ben wasn't up; Sarah Lynn walked into the bedroom, bent over and shook him several times. "Ben England, Ben England," raising her voice, "It is time to get up. The twins will be up in thirty minutes and they both will want time in the bathroom."

Ben turned over. Reaching out with one hand, he touched Sarah's leg. "Honey just five more minutes, I ache all over. Just five more . . . "

"I told you so. You take off on the weekend and leave the kids for me to take care of. Ben England it isn't fair," she said, rushing out of the room, tears running down her face.

Ben almost fell out of bed. Staggering, he reached for the wall; steadying himself before entering the bathroom to freshen up. Entering the kitchen, he reached for the chair and slowly plopped down.

"Honey, I'm sorry." Ben said, trying to smooth things.

Sarah acted like she hadn't heard a word. Continuing to stand at the stove, nonchalant to . . .

Sarah Lynn, "I'm sorry. Don't you believe me? Tell you what, why don't we get your mother to take care of the twins next Saturday. We'll take in the town; a dinner and a show.?"

Turning to face Ben, "You think you will get off that easy buster. If every other Saturday is like the last one, it will cost you plenty."

"Would you please pour me a cup of coffee?" he asked. "I'll call the store and let them know I will be a little late."

"You'll do no such thing. I'll fix your breakfast while you go and get dressed."

"Barking orders again," he said, while walking out of the kitchen. "I always loved a woman that could speak her mind and then smile while saying it."

"Get out of here Ben England."

After breakfast, Sarah told Ben she needed the car to run some errands and then meet Sue Ann for lunch. "You will have to take your truck today."

Ben and the twins headed out the door, turning to throw Sarah another kiss. The twins walked to the road and waited for the school bus, while Ben opened the door of his 68 Ford truck, a bright lipstick red, chrome wheels, big 325 motor, with a modified exhaust system that could be heard several blocks away. Turning their heads toward the roar of the engine, the twins waved at him, as he bolted out of the yard.

He smiled and waved back, before reaching for the radio knob, surfing for his favorite station. Charlie Daniels, the King of Bluegrass playing, *The Devil went down to Georgia,* as Ben bellowed the tune.

He smiled as he entered the store. Joanne walked

up to him, touched him on the shoulder and whispered, "the boss wants to see you."

Ben knocked on the door, paused, before entering the office. Jim West, the president stood to his feet and offered his hand, then motioned for Ben to have a seat.

"Ben, I have good news and bad news. Which one do you want first," he asked.

"Sir I would prefer the good news first, if it is ok with you," Ben told him. "I will try and live with the bad news."

"Ok," he said. "I have finally landed a government contract for some of our machine parts. The first order comes in next month."

"Sir, that's fantastic. You have worked hard in building the business and I am proud to be associated with the company."

"Now the bad news. You are being promoted to regional sales manager. You will be on the road a few days each month calling on military installations and other companies that need our products," pausing . . . waiting for a reply from Ben.

"I don't know what to say. It is a big advancement for me, but can I discuss this with my wife?"

"Of course, I have confidence in your ability and this would be good for your career. Let me know in a day or two?" Jim told him.

Chapter 5

Sarah Lynn set the supper table, and turned to walk into the living room, where the twins were watching cartoons and Ben was stretched out on the couch asleep. She nudged him. "Time to get up. You and the kids wash your hands while I put supper on the table." She returned to the stove and dished up fried chicken, green beans with potatoes and crumbled bacon, corn bread and milk for all four.

The kids finished first and headed back to the TV. Sonny turned and asked, "what's for dessert?"

Sarah replied, "Banana pudding with whipped cream."

"Boy mom. You are the best mom ever," he said as he hurried to turn on the TV.

"You know Sarah, the twins are right. You are the best mom and wife ever."

"Why thank you sir. You're not so bad yourself."

After supper, they sat at the table enjoying a cup of coffee. Ben was a little fidgety and found it hard to get the words out. He coughed and cleared his throat, before reaching for Sarah's hand.

"Honey, the boss called me into his office today and . . .

"What did he want this time?" she asked.

"Well I will be getting a raise. We landed a government contract for our machine products. Isn't that great news?"

"Ok, what's the punch line?" she asked. "There has to be more to it."

"Well, uh . . . Mr. West is going to make me Regional Sales Manager for the company."

"Now wait a minute. When did the company every have a region to work? Come on, spit it out, the truth," she told him.

"Honey this is a good opportunity for me to advance my career. I will only be gone a few days out of the month. I will call on military camps and other businesses that need our products."

"Only a few days a month. Ha! And what am I to do while you are gone?"

"Huh . . . there's your mother. She can help with the kids. Besides I will make more money and you can buy that new bedroom set you always wanted."

"Now you are trying to bribe me. Oh well, I guess it won't hurt to try it for awhile. You tell Mr. West this may be one unhappy girl he has to deal with, but you can go for it."

Reaching across the table, Ben kissed her. "Thanks honey. I'll help clean the table and wash the dishes."

"Ben England. You got to me again. You charmed me ten years ago and you still haven't lost it," Sarah said. She placed her arms around his neck, a passionate kiss followed. Hurry and I will meet you in the bedroom later," she winked at him.

Hurrying to get undress, he laid under the sheet waiting for Sarah to come out of the bathroom. "It sure takes her a long time to get ready for bed," he muttered.

"I heard that Ben England."

Sarah stepped out of the bathroom. Standing still in the dim light, her form filled the shear pale blue night-gown. Her long auburn brown hair; flowing over one side of her face, showcased her doe brown eyes. She smiled, while walking to the outreached hand of her husband . . . sliding under the sheet, Ben placed his right arm under her waist, gently pulling her to his chest.

Chapter 6

Ben and Joe, walking through the woods to the camp site, kept a sharp focus on their movement. Checking every move and step, Joe muttered, "There'll not be any surprises this time." When they arrived at the camp, they noticed Billie Rae was missing and another man was standing just outside the ring of fire.

"Where's Billie Ray?" Joe asked.

"It appears he washed out and wouldn't be coming back," a soldier spoke up. "We have a new recruit; his name is Tommy, Tommy Johnson. He is waiting for the Colonel to come and swear him in."

"Great to have you on board, Tommy," Ben said. Ben and Joe took turns shaking his hand and in unison spoke, "welcome to the Brigade." Joe continued, "If you like crawling like a snake, running until you drop and drinking water like a dog, then you've come to the right place," Joe said as the others broke into a hearty laugh. "Yes sir, this is the place."

"Thank you for the warm welcome," Tommy said.

Colonel Jackson stepped out of the shadows, walking toward the ring of fire. The soldiers jumped to their feet and saluted. "Sir we have a new recruit," Joe stated. This is Tommy Johnson."

"Welcome Johnson. I will swear you in after our

exercise today," Colonel Jackson told him.

"Our exercise today will include team work. Each team will have a certain territory to cover and protect. The object is to capture the flag of the opposing team and bring the flag back to camp. Now I would like to introduce you to Johnny Hawkeye. Johnny is a full blood Cherokee Indian. He will teach you some easy sign language and whistle codes that you will need during this exercise. He is a retired Army Master Sergeant and distinguished himself, along with other Cherokees, during the Korean and Vietnam War."

Hawkeye walked to the center of the ring of fire. He was nearly six feet, slender built, long black hair with a touch of gray, pulled pact in a pony tail. His eyes were piercing and the passion of his voice stirred the inner parts of our being.

The Colonel, pulling names out of a hat, told the men, each even or odd name would be on opposite sides. There was Ben, Joe, Billie Ray, Jimmy, Cecil and Carl on team A and the balance of the soldiers were on team B.

Hawkeye will take team B and spend two hours with them. Afterward he will spend two hours with team A.

Silence, silence, silence is the key to victory.

"Does anyone remember sitting on a large boulder, rifle cocked and pointed in the direction of the noise?" he asked. "Then a voice spoke, lay down your weapon, spread eagle and like the wind there was no one there."

Ben's face turned red, like a crimson rose. He wrinkled his nose and his mouth twitched, and then sheepishly raised his arm half mast.

"That's what I am talking about. Silence in every movement. You must catch your prey unaware and then strike hard and fast for the kill."

Colonel Jackson stepped forward. "At three a.m. team A will hit the trail and set up camp. At four a.m. team B will go in the opposite direction and set up camp.

Three a.m. came earlier than expected. The six men gathered around the ring of fire, where they selected Joe Capps to be their leader. Silently they moved from the camp and disappeared in the early morning fog. Joe was the point, while Ben would cover their tracks from the rear. Deep in the woods they dredged. Joe stopped. Glancing over the rough terrain, he motioned that the others could proceed. As they gathered in a circle, he told them this would be a good spot to make camp. "Cecil I want you to take the high spot on that ridge. You will be our sentry until dark. The rest of you take a fifteen minute break."

Cecil, making his way up the hill cut small branches, as he continues to move upward. When he reached the position, where his view was not hindered, he placed the branches on the ground. One by one he attached them to his clothing. Perching himself near a huge tree, he blended in with the scenery.

Scanning the ridge with his field glasses, Joe

wasn't able to make out Cecil's location. Placing his hands to his mouth, he called, "caw, caw, caw and a whistle, caw, caw, caw and a whistle."

There was a slight breeze rustling the leaves, but the responsive sound, "caw, caw, caw and a whistle came through clear."

Turning to address the men, Joe instructed them to gather branches and insert them in their clothing. "We want to blend in as we leave camp and enter the enemies territory. I want that flag."

Chapter 7

Sarah Lynn was busy at home. She had harvested a bushel of green beans, two pecks of tomatoes and six dozen ears of corn from the garden. Muttering, "I'll leave the cucumbers and squash for another day. While the kids are in school, I will call my mother and have her come and help me can."

"Mom I just finished bringing in a load of vegetables that need to be canned. Will you come over and help me?" she asked.

"Lynn, let me finish watching this program. Give me thirty minutes and I'll be there."

Sarah walked to the back porch; reached up to pull a large galvanized tub off the hook. She placed it in the sink, washing it with soap and hot water. She shucked the corn and broke up the green beans and placed them on a clean towel to dry.

Where did Ben put the Mason Jars? I believe he mentioned the shed. She walked out the kitchen door, stepping off the porch; and walked a few yards to the old wooden shed. Opening the door, a swarm of bees flew past her. She swatted at the pest, slinging her arms and hands, as some attached themselves to her clothing. Brushing them off, she yelped, and started to cry. Wiping stingers from her arms and clothes, she swore, "I'll get even with Ben England for not taking care of things."

She picked up the canning jar carton and walked briskly back to the house. Once inside the kitchen, she plopped the jars on the counter and ran cold water on her arms and brushed the water through her hair. A few bees, still on her apron were flipped to the floor, where she stepped on them and used a broom to sweep them up and discarded them in the trash can.

She opened the carton, brushed off the cob webs, and placed the jars in the tub of hot soapy water. When all the jars were cleaned, Sarah reached in the cabinet and pulled out the water bath, then the pressure canner.

A bee crawling up her arm; plunged its stinger deep in her flesh, before she flipped it. "It hurts," she yelled. "Ben England, you asked for it."

Mom knocked on the door and continues walking through the living room to the kitchen.

"Lynn, what can I do?" She asked.

"You can put the large pot on the stove; fill it with water and the green beans on the counter. We need to par boil them for about five minutes. Oh Mom, you know what to do. You taught me, so let's get busy."

"What's Ben up to now?" Mom asked.

"With a broad smile on her face, he has a new position at the company. They now have a regional sales position and Ben was selected to fill it."

"Honey that's wonderful. Do you mind if I ask a

question?" Without waiting for an answer she asked, "Does he get a raise?"

"Of course." he does. "If he didn't get one, I wouldn't let him go on the road and away from home."

"What do you mean? How often does he go out of town?" Mom asked.

"It will be several days out of the month. He will be calling on military bases and other businesses that need his products."

"Is Ben playing games again?" asked Mom.

"Of course. He is playing war games with some armchair generals. He plays with paintball guns and sometimes his uniform is colored red where he has been shot. I guess he's still a teenager at heart."

"Honey, he certainly loves you and the twins. Guess he needs some time to himself." Mom told her.

"Thanks a lot Mom. What about me? Don't I deserve some quality time to myself. I stay home, cook, clean the house, laundry and now I am in the midst of hours of canning."

"Baby, I didn't mean to upset you. I tell you what I'll do. I'll keep the twins next Friday and Saturday. I'll pay for you to have a pettiacure and hair."

"Oh Mom, I didn't mean to complain, but thanks a lot. I'll do it," she told her.

"Ben said I could buy the bedroom suit I fell in love with next month. Would you go with me?"

Chapter 8

Tuesday morning Ben drove to the Post Office to check his mail. Opening the mail box, he noticed a small brown envelope, mixed with his regular mail and several pieces of junk flyers. There was no return address on the brown envelope. He moved his fingers over it several times, muttering under his voice, "I'll wait until I get outside and check it some more." Leaving the Post Office, he placed the envelope on the front seat of the car, then pulled out from the parking lot and aimed the car to the city park. Ben picked up the envelope, slid from under the wheel and walked to a picnic table under a large Oak tree. "What's in it?" he said out loud.

Two little boys, walking by the table, asked Ben, "What are you doing?"

"For your information, I stopped under this shade tree to read my mail. Why aren't you boys in school? Ben asked.

The boys paused. "I know you. You're Sonny England's dad, one of the boys said.

"Yes, I am Sonny's daddy. What are you boys doing here in the park?" he asked.

Both boys started to run . . .

Ben gently pulled the tape from one side, then the other. He opened the envelope and slid the CD out.

"What is this?" he murmured. I guess I will find out soon enough, walking back to the car and inserting the CD in the slot. Listening carefully, a man's voice spoke, "this is your assignment. For security reasons it shares only one half of the details of one person that is involved in the destruction of our freedom and liberty. We must eradicate the enemy within our midst. You will be contacted by your partner within three days for the other part of the message and the name of the individual. This CD will self destruct as soon as you eject the disk."

Ben lowered his head, "am I doing the right thing, God? I want to save my country, but destroying another life . . . "is that the right thing to do?" I'll read my Bible when I get home. Maybe there's an answer to my dilemma.

After dinner Ben turned the television off and strode to the front door. Staring at the moon, watching it moved in and out of the gray floating clouds. A strong wind rustled the leaves on the large oak tree. "It looks like a story is brewing," he murmured.

Random thoughts ran through his head. "Am I doing the right thing?"

Sarah Lynn finished cleaning the kitchen and walked into the living room. Noticing the television was off, she made her way to the door, placing her arms around Ben's waist. "What's wrong? You are quiet and moody tonight." "Nothing to speak of," Ben replied. "What was the sermon about at church Sunday?"

"Well, huh, let me think a moment. Oh, now I re-member. The pastor preached on *The Good Samaritan.* How we should treat one another and our neighbor."

"Thanks honey. I will try and remember that," he answered. "How were the children over the weekend? Did your mother come over and help with the canning?"

"Yes she did. And she is going to take the twins next weekend. She also loves me so much that she is go-ing to splurge for a new hairdo, nails and pedicure."

"That's wonderful. Your mother is something else. Did you tell her you were going to buy a new bedroom suit? You know, the one you always wanted?"

"Absolutely. She's going to the furniture store with me. By the way, next week is free and I want a date with you. I want dinner and a movie, so plan on it now."

Chapter 9

Tuesday morning, Ben left the house and drove by the coffee shop, ordered a cup of special blend coffee, and aimed the car to the city park. He parked his car, taking a couple more sips of coffee, while watching through the mirror for Joe to enter the lot. Noticing Joe's vehicle enter; Ben slid out of the front seat and walked toward the restroom facilities, a cinder block building with the usual toilet and a couple urinals. He entered and leaned against the far wall, waiting for Joe.

After making his exit from his car, Joe walked toward the building, carrying a small package. Entering the restroom, he looked around, opening each stall door. "Never can be too careful," he told Ben.

"I agree. What's in the package?" Ben asked.

Joe opened the package, revealing a picture of an Arab man and some of his colleagues. "This is the target," he said. "This man is heading one the largest Muslim Brotherhood organizations in America. He has access to the President and even some of his fellow Muslims are in high government jobs, like Homeland Security.

"Why is he our target?" Ben asked.

"That's a foolish question Ben. Anyone that wants to destroy our freedom and liberty is an enemy of America. Besides, I don't ask questions."

"Did you receive the other half of our job?"

"Yes. We need to figure out when?"

Dr. Aluah will be the major speaker at the Council on American Islamic Relations next Thursday at the Radisson Hotel in Atlanta. This is an inter-community relations briefing; bringing different faiths, law officers, community leaders and politicians together so that they can have a better understanding of Islam and the Muslim community. Dr. Aluah is quite influential on the Hill and has been in the White House many times. His influence has advocated a change in the CIA and FBI manuals on terrorism. No longer are they allowed to use the words; jihad and terrorist in referring to Muslims or the Islamic faith.

"You need to take a late flight to Atlanta on Tuesday," Joe told him. "I'll drive to Knoxville, pick up a rental car, and I will meet you at the Atlanta airport. There's a small motel on the out skirts of town. We will check in, devise our plans and make preparations a day in advance."

Monday morning, Ben entered the office and stopped at the receptionist desk. "I have a sales meeting with a small weapons company in Athens, Georgia. I'll be out of town for a couple days. I'll fill in all the details when I get back."

Tuesday afternoon Ben boarded the plane in Knoxville at five, making the short one hour flight to

Atlanta. He wandered through the airport, with his lone carryon and walked to the waiting area for Joe. Sitting for some twenty minutes, Ben pulled out a pen and pad, scribbled a few lines, then drawing some figures, when his thoughts turned to the weekend. "What a great time I had with Sarah. She is a keeper."

Walking through the sliding doors, Joe looked to the left and then to the right, finding Ben with his head down and scribbling on the pad. "What's this?" Joe asked.

"Nothing much. Just thinking about Sarah and the kids. Joe you should get married. It's a great life if you don't weaken," he said, grinning.

"I thought about it a couple times. Got cold feet and I've been a loner all my life," Joe said.

"When we get back, I could fix you up with one of Sarah's friends. What do you think of that? We could double date."

Joe laughed. "Let's get out of here."

They left the airport. Traveling on a side street to their destination, they stopped at a fast food joint, ordered four cheeseburgers, fries and two large drinks. Sipping on the drinks, they would wait until they checked in the motel before eating.

Joe pulled into the parking lot. Glancing at the motel and surrounding buildings, it was idea. The motel was non-descript, off the beaten path in the shady part of the city. He opened the door to the office, pushed the small bell several times before a man with long hair pulled back into a pony tail approached from the back room. Joe took a quick glance through the open door, viewing beer bottles and WWE wrestling on the TV.

The night clerk cleared his throat, "room for the night," he asked.

"Maybe a couple nights . . .

"That will be $48.00 for the two nights. Cash only." Joe pulled two twenties and a ten spot from his pocket and picked up the pen to fill out the form. Looking up, Joe asked, "who's winning the wrestling match?"

"Don't matter to me. Not much on TV so I just like to see them bust heads or watch the women . . . now there are some real lookers," he said.

Joe laughed. "What time do you close the office?"

"We shut down around ten, but sometimes a customer will come in for a few hours. You know what I mean . . . it's none of my business."

Joe picked up the key to room 337, located on the end of the motel. Once inside, he closed the blinds and opened the door to let Ben in, carrying the burgers and drinks. "This is idea. There's not a desk manger, night clerk or anyone to monitor our in and out." Joe said. "Tomorrow morning we will drive by the hotel, survey the area and decide the best position and opportunity to take care of business."

"What are you interested in viewing on TV?" Ben asked.

"Let's see if they have any reruns of '24'. I always

liked that program or even NCIS is another one."

Ben, flipping through the channels, finally stopped at channel 125. "NCIS is on for two hours. Let's watch one and then try and find 24."

Joe, stretching out on the bed, placed the two pillows together and leaned back against the head board.

Ben made his way to a chair next to his side of the bed, sitting back with his arms behind his head, watching NCIS. It was after ten when they both retired for the night.

Early the next morning, before daylight, Ben walked out the door, heading to the coffee shop nearby. He picked up two cups of coffee. On the way back to the motel, he noticed several police cars, with their lights flashing, down the street. "I wonder what's that all about," muttering to himself.

When he reached the motel door, he kicked with his foot, tapping several times before Joe peeping through the blinds let him in.

"What was all the noise about?" Joe asked.

"I'm not sure, but it looks like someone broke into a parts store in the next block," Ben said. Joe slid the blinds back enough to see out . . . backing up from the window as two plain black cars entered the parking lot. Four men slid out of the cars, rushed to the office. "What now?" he exclaimed.

Seeing the four men, he turned to Ben, telling him to pick up his stuff and go to the bathroom. If they come to the door I'll handle it.

There was a loud noise, like gun shots, coming from somewhere close to their room. Cracking the door to get a better look, Joe noticed several police cars entering the motel lot. Again, there were several more gun shots. Joe closed the door, locking it. Standing back from the door, waiting for someone to knock, his heart and pulse were racing. Feeling uneasy, Joe sat down on the side of the bed. Hearing the rumble noise outside, he jumped to his feet and quickly walked to the window. Cracking the blinds, he saw a police cruiser with a man and a woman in the back seat. Showing a sigh of relief, he called Ben to come out. They both looked at each other and drew a deep breath.

Joe casually walked to his car. Looking around, he noticed the coroner's van was parked outside a door. Two officers carried a body bag out, placing it in the van. Joe opened the trunk and picked up some papers before he strode back inside.

"Ok partner, let's get out of here," he said. "Besides, I'm hungry as a bear waking up from his winter nap." Both men entered the car. Joe slid under the wheel and pulled out of the parking lot onto Magnolia Avenue. Driving the speed limit, Ben spotted a hole in the wall café. "Let's eat here?"

Joe made the right turn and parked in the back parking lot. "I hope this is not a greasy spoon," Ben remarked. They made their exit and walked to the side door of the café. A waitress motioned for them to take a seat by the wall. When she came to the table, "are you ready to order? May I suggest, "sausage, eggs and biscuits with gravy over the top." Ben, looking up from the menu asked, "Is the gravy brown or white? You know the white kind that comes out of a can."

She smiled and replied, "Sugar, I'll make it any color you want, brown or white. Now that we got that settled, how do you like your eggs?"

Joe spoke up, "I like my eggs," with a snicker.

"I like them too, but do you want them sunny side up or scrambled?" she asked.

"Whoever heard of scrambled eggs with gravy?" asked Ben. "I'll take mine sunny side up and could you add a couple slices of tomato"

Joe piped in. "Make that two of the same, with brown gravy."

Chapter 10

Sarah Lynn had the twins bathed and in the car when Ben drove up. "Where are you going with the kids?" he asked.

"Ben I am taking the kids to mother for the weekend. Don't you remember tonight is our date night?" she told him, twitching her nose and staring at him.

"Of course I remember. I was just playing along to see if you remembered. I'll go in and freshen up. I'll be ready by the time you get back."

Sarah Lynn slammed the car door. She hit the pedal, making the tires spin as she drove off. Saying out loud, "I don't understand men."

Ben walked into the house, heading to the bathroom to shave and freshen up. He also thought to himself, "Boy, I got out of that one."

Sarah spent a few minutes at her mothers home, letting her know what time to put the twins to bed and what shows on TV they could watch. She kissed her mother and the twins and out the door she ran. When she arrived at home, Ben was almost ready. She jumped at him. "Not so fast Mr. England, you thought you pulled a good one on me. I am used to your schnagians."

Ben quickly put his arms around her, pulled her close and kissed her . . . passionately. Backing up, "what were you saying?" he asked.

"You big lug, let's get out of here." hitting him on the shoulder. Ben locked the door, ushered Sarah by the arm to the car, and then opened the door for her to slide in.

"Thank you," she said.

Ben walked to the driver's side and hopped under the wheel. "Where too my fair lady?" he asked.

"We are dining at the Smokehouse and I want BBQ ribs and everything that goes with it," she told him. "Afterward we are going to the movies. I don't care what's playing. I want some time with my husband."

Ben opened the door to the Smokehouse, letting Sarah enter first. The Smokehouse was known throughout the county for their award winning BBQ. The décor was simple backwoods, with wood shavings on the floor, dim lights and a long bar trimmed in brass. The walls were rough peck cedar inlaid, showcasing fishing and hunting scenes and various country singers. In one corner sat an old juke box, brightly lit and ready for a quarter to be inserted. On stage was a young man singing, Billie Rae Cyrus hit song; Achy, Breaky Heart.

Ben started to sing along, when Sarah punched him in the ribs. The hostess, turning her head, smiled and continued to walk in front of them to a table toward the back. Walking close to the wall, they viewed the pictures of various country western singers, some which had been autographed. "I know most all of the singers," Sarah said.

I have many of their old 78 records."

Ben pulled the straight back wood chair from the table, allowing Sarah to sit, then walked to the opposite side and took his seat. When the waitress appeared, Ben ordered the house special, a large platter of ribs, baked potato, salad and rolls. Sarah ordered the petite plate of ribs, baked potato and salad.

"It has been months, moisture formed in her eyes, since we have had time alone. I hope with this new job we can do this more often. Mom doesn't mind keeping the children and besides we need some good times, too."

Chewing on a rib bone, Ben shook his head up and down. He wiped his mouth with a napkin and . . . "I agree, we must do this more often."

He started to sing the little jingle, "If you've got the money honey, I've got the time."

Sarah stared at him.

Ben lowered his head, "Can't a guy have a little fun with his chick? Listen Sarah, the band is playing one of your favorite songs. Want to cut a rug," reaching her hand, helping her stand and walk to the dance floor.

She snuggled up close to his chest, wrapping her arms around his neck and slowly moved around the floor.

"Hey good looking, why don't we skip the movie and head home," she said.

"You mean more surprises . . ." he asked.

"You'll never know . . ."

Chapter 11

General Boyd was busy with the new recruits in Florida. They had gathered on the outskirts of the Everglades and would spend their training period in the Glades. Twenty of Florida's finest sharp shooters were present to listen to the rousing and emotional speech from the General.

In his opening remarks, the General talked about freedom and liberty. He mentioned the 57 founding fathers of this great nation and the sacrifice they made to break away from the mother country and became a free and independent nation. He read the first and second Amendments to the Constitution. At the end of his speech to the twenty gators, there was a standing applause. "Men I want to introduce you to Colonel Jackson. Colonel Jackson will outline our agenda in brief terms and pair each one of you with another Gator," he told them.

Colonel Jackson walked a few steps out of the shadows and addressed the men. He outlined the agenda and what was expected of each volunteer. "Gentleman you are in for some tough training in the 'Glades.' I will give you a list of the things you will need to bring to our next meeting in two weeks."

One hand from the group was raised in the air.

"What is your question?" asked the Colonel.

"Sir how long will this mission be?" he asked.

"Soldier if you don't wash out, it will last until the mission is complete," he said. "How long depends on the enemy, both foreign and domestic."

"We have several other states involved in the Brigade and some of them are already on assignments. Don't be alarmed when you read the newspaper or listen to the evening news. We are starting to take back our country."

As the men were sitting around the ring of fire, one spoke up. "I've never been in the Everglades. That thing is a swamp." When he said swamp, some of the men smiled and some even snickered. Billy Bob looked at the others and said, "I've made a living out of that swamp. However, there are poisonous snakes, alligators and other prey just waiting for a sample."

The men didn't seem amused at that statement.

Colonel Jackson passed out a sheet of paper with all the necessary items the men needed to bring for their next meeting. "We will meet in two weeks from today at 6 in the morning. Be prepared for a full day's workout in the swamp."

He continued, "The Brigade is a secret order of counter terrorism men which want to take back our country. I expect you to honor the code."

Chapter 12

Joe watched Ben finish the last bite of breakfast, using the last piece of the biscuits to sop the remaining gravy. They emptied their coffee cup with two sips. Ben pulled out a ten spot to leave for a tip when Joe reached his arm and told him no. "We will not leave anything that could draw attention. Just leave twenty percent and tell her how much you enjoyed the brown gravy."

They pulled out of the parking lot onto Magnolia Avenue traveling southeast toward downtown Atlanta. It was a cloudy day and the forecast was rain on and off until midnight. A huge storm was brewing in the Atlantic which could bring torrents of water during the week.

Sprinkles of rain hit the windshield.

Ben mentioned, "This could be good for us today and tomorrow. All the security will be covered, protecting themselves from the rain, and not paying attention to their surroundings."

Joe responded by shaking his head up and down, keeping his eyes on the traffic and stayed several cars behind the one in front of him.

"Hey Joe, do you remember Hannibal Smith and the 'A' Team program. I always liked to hear Hannibal say, "I like it when a plan comes together."

Joe laughed. "Well, our plan will come together

tomorrow morning."

Joe parked the car about a mile from the Radisson Hotel. Both men surveyed their surroundings before walking the short distance to the Hotel. Ben, walking behind Joe, skipped a couple steps and was even with him. "This is like hunting back home. Almost like staking out a deer and waiting for the kill," Ben said.

Joe smiled, but had to agree with Ben. "There's excitement and a rush when you go hunting," Joe said.

Nearing the Hotel, they passed a ladies boutique; showing some fancy sheer nightwear, a tobacco shop, with the aroma of cigar smoke blending in with the slight breeze rustling through the small sidewalk trees, and other small businesses. A three story brick office building was directly across from the Hotel. A sign hanging in the window advertised it was for rent or lease. "Looks like this might fill the bill," Joe said. "Let's walk around back." They moved down the side street; entering the alley in the back of the building, there were small windows and a fire escape, which looked like it had seen its last days. "Not much here to help us," Ben said. "We need a hook rod and a long rope."

Standing, they gazed down the alley, then looking up at the third story, they agreed that this was the perfect spot for the ambush. They walked to the front of the building, down past the cigar store and boutique. Both men stood for a moment and gazed at the display in the window. Ben laughed. "Sarah would look enticing in that outfit."

"Come on Ben. Quit daydreaming. You'll be home soon," Joe said.

Returning to their motel, Joe pulled out a yellow note pad, sketching the brick building, alley entrance and the strategy for the next morning. "I'll be the sniper on the second floor, while you will make a diversion several blocks away," he told Ben. "After I enter the building; you must make a big explosion so there's panic with people running in every direction."

In the cloak of darkness, Joe and Ben made their way to the brick office building across the street from the entrance to the Radisson. Using a hook and rope they purchased from Ace Hardware, Ben pulled the fire escape ladder down, allowing Joe to reach the first rung. Pulling himself up, Joe made his way to a door at the top.

Ben jumped in the car, shifted gears and sped down the alley. He made a left turn on Peachtree Boulevard and parked the car. Sitting in the car he muttered, "The hardest thing to do is sitting and waiting."

Sit and wait.

It would be nearly seven hours before Dr. Aluah and his Council of American Islamic Relations team make their exit from the Hotel.

A clap of thunder rolled like logs through the morning clouds. Then a streak of lightning flashed across the window, lighting up the whole room. Joe opened the suitcase, reached inside and pulled out the stock and barrel. In the darkness, he put the pieces together. Cocking the weapon, he pulled the trigger, hearing the firing pin snap and knew it was ready to do the job. He walked toward the back wall, sitting down and leaned against it.

His mind flashed back to the times he assumed this position, when hunting for ducks or even waiting patiently for a deer to come into view.

Lightning flashed, lighting up the room, then a clap of thunder . . . kaboom, as heavy drops of water hit against the window. Joe immediately stood to his feet. In the darkness, he walked to the window, looking at the heavy black clouds. The heavens appeared to be 'pitch black', while the rain was coming down in buckets.

Joe pressed his face against the window, "This is going to be easy," he murmured.

Meanwhile, Ben left the car, covering his head, rushed to a nearby Starbuck and ordered a cup of coffee. Walking out the door, Ben pulled the collar up around his neck, pulled the cap down and made a quick turn around the corner to enter the alley. He pushed up the lid of a large trash bin, noticing it was filled with paper, cardboard boxes and some grease from a nearby restaurant. "This will do the trick." he murmured to himself. He looked at his watch, showing eleven fifty.

Joe rose from the back wall, taking his position at the open window. He focused the weapons sight on the target across the street. Making a couple minor adjustments, he muttered, "ready."

Leaning over the trash bin, Ben struck a match, setting the papers on fire. He stepped back, after placing a prop to hold the door open, watching the flames reach the grease. Like roman candles, flames shot through the air. Pulling several bullets from his jacket, Ben tossed them in the burning inferno and swiftly walked to his car.

It was twelve fifteen, when Dr. Albui and his group walked through the glass doors of the Hotel. Pulling his raincoat collar up, Dr. Albui lowered his head, while walking to the waiting limousine.

One flash and a loud noise, like thunder, broke the stillness of time. Dr. Albui fell to the sidewalk. Many of his group rushed to cover his body, noticing the blood flowing from the wound. With all the commotion sur-rounding the Doctor, many attendees ran for cover.

Joe closed the window, unfolded the weapon and placed it in the case before running down the fire escape, dropping to the floor below. He ran swiftly down the al-ley. Finding Ben, he opened the trunk and shoved the weapon in. Both men made a quick exit, and ran toward the Hotel to access the situation. Police officers were pushing the on lookers back, while a fire truck and ambu-lance arrived on the scene. Ben and Joe standing along side the rest of the crowd, watched the paramedics work on the Doctor.

One looked up and shook his head. "He's gone."

As the crowd dispersed, Joe and Ben swiftly walked down the street to their car. Sitting in the car, they watched a police cruiser and fire truck rushing to the side street and alley. "I guess that takes care of business," Ben said. Pulling out of the lot onto Magnolia Avenue, he aimed the car to the motel.

Joe wiped his face with a cloth. Starring out the window, he lowered his voice, "It was so much more horrible than killing a deer, rabbit or a squirrel."

"I know what you mean," Ben said. "Do you remember the words of General Boyd, when he mentioned the 57 foundering fathers of this great nation, and the price they paid for our freedom and liberty?"

Joe, shaking his head continued to stare out the window.

BREAKING NEWS!

Ben and Joe were on their way home when a news flash came across the radio station they were listening to. Ben reached over, turning up the volume.

Breaking News —

Homeland Security Director killed. Janice Napes, the director of Homeland Security was assassinated today in Texas. She was in El Paso, Texas inspecting the border. The Director has been under extreme fire over her blunders with the TSA and her continued fight with border agents and the administrations light treatment of the Islamic Muslim Brotherhood. The President will give a report in the Rose Garden tomorrow morning at ten. Now back to our regular scheduled program.

"WOW! Did you hear that? Do you think it was one of our Brigades?" turning his head to look at the expression on Joe's face.

Joe was quiet and motionless, holding both hands on the steering wheel.

"What do you think?" Ben asked. "Talk to me."

In a somber tone, "I guess we are in this to the bitter end. Now drop the questions and let's get back to Knoxville and home."

Ben laid his head back, closing his eyes.

Checking his rearview mirror, Joe noticed a red light blinking behind him. He pulled over to the side of the road, turned the engine off and placed his hands on the steering wheel.

"Wake up Ben." Ben reacted quickly.

"Just place your hands on the dashboard. There's an officer approaching my side of the car."

Ben placed his hands on the dashboard, as the officer walked to the driver's side with his hand on his weapon.

"Good morning," the Officer said. "Where are you boys from?"

"We're from Bell County Kentucky sir," Joe said. Pulling his driver's license out of his billfold, "This is a rental car we are taking back to Knoxville."

"Let me see your license and the rental agreement?" asked the Officer.

"They are in the glove compartment," Ben stated. Moving his right hand down off the dash, he opened the door and pulled the rental agreement out, handing them to Joe. The Officer viewed the papers. "Ok boys, when you turn in the vehicle be sure and tell the company they have a tail light out. Have a safe trip."

"Thank you officer," Joe said. He slowly moved from the side of the road, picking up speed to enter the Interstate. His eyes were still peeled on the cruiser in his rearview mirror.

"I'm glad that turned out ok," Ben said, wiping the sweat from his brow.

"I'm glad he didn't give us a ticket. We are going to have to be more careful," Joe said.

Ben, with his feet stretched out, touching the top of the dashboard, started singing some of his favorite country songs. After a couple songs, Joe began to howl like a hound.

"What's wrong with you?" Ben asked.

"Turn the radio on and let's listen to some real music," Joe told him.

Ben flipped through the channels and stopped when he heard the beginning of a story from Atlanta.

The FBI and the Department of Justice along with the local police are investigating the murder of Dr. Abuli of the Counsel of American Islamic Relations as an assassination and a hate crime. Law enforcers are crawling all over the Radisson Hotel and local businesses on both sides of the avenue. The fire in the trash bin that exploded is also under tight security and investigation.

FBI spokesperson, Don George, Jr. gave the local Channel 9 a personal update. "It appears for now, that the person we are looking for was in the brick building across the street. There were some telltale signs, which I can not disclose at this time, for it is still an ongoing investigation."

Ben turned pale. "Did you hear that, Joe? What do you make of that FBI's comments?"

"Don't worry about it buddy, there's nothing there to indicate the killer was in that building."

"Why did the FBI indicate they had some evidence, but couldn't release it?" Ben asked.

"Relax. Relax."

"There was only one shot, one shot that broke through the black clouds and heavy rain and I picked up the shell. The man had to say something, to show that they were on top of the killing . . . understand!"

"Sit back and relax, we're on our way home." Joe said. "Close your eyes and think of Sarah Lynn, that should calm you down."

Ben chuckled.

Closing his eyes, he dozed off.

Clipping along, Joe crossed the Tennessee River and made his way to the business center of town. "Wake up Ben, we are close to the rental company."

Joe pulled into the driveway of the rental company and quickly make his exit. Ben slowly moved from the passenger side and opened the truck to pull out the bags.

After checking the rental or any damage, the clerk signed off on the rental, and thanked them for their business.

"I almost forgot, one of the taillights is not working." Joe told him.

Chapter 13

Saturday was the twins seventh birthday and Sarah was planning a party in the back yard that would include a portable jumper. She had already baked the birthday cake; putting pink icing on one half and blue of the other, and decorated the pink with fairy story figurines and on the blue side, she placed cowboys and Indians.

"I can't wait for Ben to come home," she muttered. "He better show up for this party. Two or three days are just too much."

Opening the front door, Ben walked slowly toward the kitchen. Standing still in the doorway, he glanced, with a raised eye brow, at Sarah busy washing dishes. Tiptoeing, Ben slowly made his way to her back, reaching down he kissed her on the back of her neck.

She squealed. "Cut that out, my husband will be in shortly."

"Your husband?"

"Why, it's you Ben," Sarah laughed.

Turning, with suds still on her hands, she placed her arms around his neck, kissing him again and again. "I am so glad you're home."

"What can I do to help?" he asked.

"First of all, tell me about your trip. Was it successful?" she asked.

"Yes it was successful. We took care of business."

"I was worried about you. The news said there was a killer on the loose in Atlanta. He killed some doctor. I wanted you safe and sound," her eyes swelled with tears.

Ben kissed the tears flowing down her face. "I am home now honey. I am safe and I love you more each day," pulling her close to his chest.

He could feel the rapid beat of her heart against his body. He stepped back and let her tend to her face. Ben stood there looking at Sarah, then watching her walk out of the kitchen to the bathroom to freshen up.

When she returned, she hit him on the shoulder. "You big lug, I love you too."

"Did you and your mother buy the bedroom out-fit?"

"Let's walk to the bedroom," she said.

Ben took one look. He fell on the bed, lay back and stretched out. He wiggled his index finger at Sarah and invited her next to him. Sarah walked a few steps, turned and flopped on the bed next to him. He placed his left arm over her waist, kissing her deeply . . .

"Not now," she said. "The children will be home from school."

Ben laughed. "Just like a practical woman," sliding out of bed. Laughing, they walked out of the bedroom, hand in hand.

In the kitchen, Sarah put a fresh pot of coffee on

the stove, then reached in the cupboard and pulled out a pound cake. "The strawberries are in the refrigerator. Please get the for me?" she asked Ben.

"Honey do you remember Joe Capps? I would like to invite him to the birthday party. He's single and I was telling him about some of your girl friends."

Sarah laughed. "Which one do you have in mind?"

"Well, he's good looking, almost as good looking as . . . I was thinking of Shirley Jean. Did you invite her?"

"Well it is a kid's party. No I didn't invite Shirley. I will call and see if she will come."

"You've had a busy day. Why don't I pick up a pizza for dinner? I'll make a good salad to go with it," he told her.

The twins departed the school bus, running to see who could get in the house first. Bonnie screamed as Sonny closed the door in her face. She opened the door. Seeing her dad she ran across the room and jumped in his arms. Ben picked her up, round and round, so much that both of them were dizzy.

"Daddy, we are having a birthday party tomorrow. I am so excited. I want a Barbie doll, clothes and a new pair of skates," she told him. Sonny piped in with his request, "I want a basketball."

"Let's see what happens tomorrow."

Saturday afternoon.

Eight children were bouncing up and down in the

jumper, screaming, laughing and making funny noises. The adults were sitting at a picnic table drinking sweet tea and munching on chips and dip. Joe Capps, the handsome partner of Ben wore a baseball cap, with a big "T" on the front covering his long blond hair, made his way around the side of the house. Ben stood up and walked to meet him. He introduced Joe to the adults and pushed Joe toward the empty seat next to Shirley. She blushed, as she reached for the chip bowl and passed it to Joe. Sarah poured a large glass of ice tea for him.

The conversation was light hearted with a lot of laughter.

Sonny jumped down from the jumper. Mama, mama, "is it time to open the presents?"

"Almost honey. Let me go in the house and get them."

Chapter 14

After a fun weekend, a birthday party and introducing Joe to Shirley, Ben wasn't quite ready to go to work. Dropping by the Post Office to check his mail, he pulled out junk advertising, discarding it in the small trash container next to the table. "Nothing good or bad today," he muttered. On his way to the office, he shook the thoughts from his head, the murder of the CAIR official in Atlanta. Feeling ill in his stomach, Ben wiped his brow with a hankie and continues driving to work. Entering the Company parking lot, he picked up his briefcase, slid from under the wheel and walked slowly to the front entrance of the building. Pausing, he opened the door. Standing in his office doorway, the owner motioned for Ben to come to the office. "Are you ok?" He asked. "You look ill."

"I'm ok. I must be coming down with a bug," Ben said.

"Give me the scoop on your trip."

Ben stuttered for a moment. Opening his briefcase, he pulled out an order sheet. "It looks like we we'll have this sewed up by the end of the month. I just need to confirm with the purchasing agent how many they are good for."

"Great work Ben. That's a good start for a new

Regional Manager."

"Thank you sir. I hope to call on more businesses and make our company one of the top producers for the Armed Services and many manufacturing plants."

Ben walked out of the office, heading to his office in the middle of the building. As he entered, his telephone was ringing. Reaching across the desk he picked up the phone. "This is Ben England. How may I help you?"

The phone went dead.

Ben walked out of his office. Heading to the receptionist desk, he muttering, "Who could that be on the phone?" He stopped at the desk, asking Marge if the call he just received came through the switchboard.

"I haven't any calls for you this morning," she said.

Walking back to his office, he closed the door. "Who or what does that mean . . . a call, then the phone. He pulled the chair away from the desk, sitting down, he pondered, "who or what does that mean?" Ben picked up the phone and dialed Joe. "Joe did you just call me?" he asked.

"Not today," he replied.

"I just receive a phone call a couple minutes ago and when I answered, the line went dead."

Joe laughed. "You're on pins and needles? I told you not to worry. Look, let's get together Saturday morning for coffee?"

"I can't this Saturday. I have some things to do

with Sarah and the kids," Ben told him. "Sarah was after me this morning. She wanted to know what you thought of Shirley Jean. You can come clean with me. I won't say a word, except to Sarah, for she will surely put the bite on me."

"Well, pausing to ponder the question, I think she was nice. She had a nice smile and a good sense of humor. Who knows what will happen?" he laughed.

"How about double dating. We could go to the movies. Ben told him. "Give me a call and I will have Sarah get in touch with Shirley."

"Let me check my calendar. You know single guys are usually busy and booked," laughing.

"Ok. I'll call you later. I have some paper work to complete and turn in," Ben said.

After dinner, Ben and Sarah relaxed over a cup of vanilla nut coffee. "I talked with Joe and he thought Shirley was nice and even had a good sense of humor. Can you image that?"

"Well, she is cute, nice and does have a good sense of humor." Sarah growled at Ben. "Who are you? Ok, you are handsome and have a sense of humor but nice is another question!"

"Ok, guess I needed that. I tell you what. I'll be nice if you can convince Shirley to double date. How is that smarty?"

Chapter 15

Colonel Jackson stood before the Brigade, congratulating each member for a job well done.

"I want to commend two of our sharp shooters, without mentioning any names, for attending to detail. Many of you have read in the papers about the murder of the doctor in Atlanta and also the HLS Director in El Paso. This is the start of our revolution in taking back our country."

One of the patriots raised his hand and asked, "What are our future plans?"

Colonel Jackson raised his voice and responded, "We have a list of domestic and foreign targets that include terrorist, progressives, administration officials, judges, cabinet members, czars and could also include the White House."

The White House. "Did I hear you right?" one member asked.

"Absolutely. The President in 2009 gave a speech where he outlined FEMA Camps that would incarcerate American citizens from one year up to ten years just for thinking of a revolution or any actions deemed rebellion against the establishment. Mind you this is against our Constitution. The President has flushed it down the toilet. For a number of years we have been sold a bill of goods.

We, the Brigade, will not become another Ruby Ridge, Waco, Texas or Benghazi."

"What do you mean by Ruby Ridge and Waco, Texas?" another member asked the Colonel.

"I could explain both of these but I want you to go home and Google Ruby Ridge and Waco. We will discuss those events at our next meeting."

Ben and Joe, walking out of the woods, aimed their bodies toward home. "I don't remember anything about Ruby Ridge, do you Joe?" asked Ben. "I guess it was way before our time. I remember hearing about the Davidian massacre in Waco, Texas under the Clinton administration. Janet Reno was the Attorney General at that time and it was a mess. Something you wouldn't think the government capable of doing, especially in a free country."

Joe entered his apartment and threw the gear on a chair. He made his way to the refrig and pulled out a Bud. He took a couple swallows before walking to the small table holding his computer. Turning the computer on, he typed in the words Ruby Ridge. His eyes popped and his heart sunk, reading post after post and watching an old U-Tube video of the encounter. Randy Weaver, a white separatist, had been targeted by the federal government after failing to appear in court to face charges related to his selling of two illegal sawed-off shotguns to an Alcohol, Tobacco and Firearms (ATF) informant. On August

21, 1992, after a period of surveillance, U. S. Marshals came upon Harris, Weaver's 14 year old son Sammy and the family dog, Striker, on a road near the Weaver property. A marshal shot and killed the dog, prompting Sammy to fire at the marshal. In the ensuing gun battle, Sammy and U.S. Marshal Michael Degan were killed. A tense standoff ensued, and on August 22, the FBI joined the marshals besieging Ruby Ridge, the home and property of Randy Weaver.

Later in the day, Harris, Weaver and his daughter, Sarah left the cabin to prepare the body of Samuel for burial. As they walked out of the cabin, a sharp shooter, Lon Horiuchi, waiting 200 yards away, opened fire, wounding Weaver. The three attempted to escape back into the cabin, when a volley for fire from Horiuchi's weapon, wounding Harris, but killing Vicki Weaver, who was holding the door open with one hand and cradling her infant daughter with the other. The intense standoff, lasting over a week, when finally Harris, Weaver and Weaver's three daughters surrendered to authorizes. In 1993, Weaver and Harris were acquitted by a federal court on murder, conspiracy and other charges related to Degan's death.

Joe felt sick!

Rubbing his hands over his face, he rose from the computer, walking away and growling to himself. With mist in his eyes, and his mind racing, "how can this be?" Our government, so corrupt and cruel, wiping out a whole family. Walking into the small kitchen, Joe opened the refrigerator, pulling out another beer. Standing at the window, he stared into space . . . "why, why, why."

He picked up the phone and dialed Ben. There was no answer. Hanging up, Joe flopped down on the small brown couch, downing what was left in the beer bottle. He rose from the couch and walked to the front door. Opening the door he slammed it behind him and continued walking off the wood porch into the yard. Grabbing the bottle, he threw it as hard as he could, hearing it break into a thousand pieces.

He began to scream.

A neighbor came running out of his apartment and seeing Joe all bent over on the ground. "Joe what in the world is the matter with you? Are you sick? Are you sick?" he asked. "Are you in pain?"

"Sick. Yes I am sick. Sick, sick, sick. Just leave me alone," Joe told him. "I'll be alright in a few minutes."

"Whatever you say, I'll be in my apartment if you need me," the neighbor told him.

Joe bent over, his head touching the ground, tears flowed down his face, and small water drops fell to the ground.

Chapter 16

Dallas-Fort Worth

Captain William Nix, leader of the Brigade in Dallas-Fort Worth checked the tape he just picked up from the Post Office. One half of the mystery, a picture, was revealed. On the back were the words of a prominent global financier. Captain Nix and his partner, Billy Dean, would collaborate together on this assignment.

Billy Dean, a Green Beret, standing 6' 2", 190 pounds of solid steel, crew cut, was recently discharged from the Army. Dean, having spent three tours in Iraq and Afghanistan, was one of the finest snipers in the battalion with 127 kills.

Using a cell phone to set up a meeting with Captain Nix, he made the call. "Sir, this is BD. What is your code?" "My code is . . ." Captain Nix replied.

"Ok sir, we will meet in the parking lot at the Dallas Tyler Galleria Wednesday morning at ten. I will be wearing a red baseball cap with the initial TC."

Wednesday morning; Dean and Nix walked through the entrance to the Mall, smelling the aroma of fresh baked Cinnamon Buns, they turned toward that direction. When the gate was lifted, Nix and Dean bought coffees and two Cinnamon buns.

Captain Nix pointed to the small table in the

corner, "let's sit there and I will share what information I have."

Nix pulled the envelope out of his jacket and removed the contents. Lying it face down on the table, he waited for Dean to do the same. Dean pulled the envelope from the notebook and removed the contents. He flipped it on the table next to Nix's, waiting for the next move.

Picking up Dean's info, Captain Nix turned it over. Dean did the same with Nix's, showing a picture of Georg Staples, the global financier. The data on the back of both pieces gave a run down on some of his activities, supporting the progressives, unions, Move-On and many organizations with an agenda to destroy America's wealth. If you need more information, Google his name and read of his rags to riches and how he accomplished it. He is your target. When you touch this picture together, it will disappear in 10 seconds.

Nix and Dean discarded the coffee and leftover buns and walked out of the Mall. They entered Dean's car and drove to the Perfect Ground Coffee Shop, where they ordered two small cups of flavored coffee. Sipping on the coffee, Dean plugged in his I-Pad to surf the internet for Georg Staples. When Staple's name came up, Dean turned it around to share the contents with Captain Nix.

"This is one wicked sick bastard," Nix said. "I believe he would sell his mother if there was a profit to be made. Look at this one. Here's a picture of Staples with the Muslim Grand Mullah. They were in cahoots with the

Germans during World War II." Looking at the picture, Dean smiled, "as they say here in Texas, you're about to meet your Alamo."

"What's his agenda and schedule for next week or two?" Nix asked.

Dean pulled up his web page. "He will make two appearances next week, one in Austin and the other one in Houston. I think the one in Houston will be the easiest one."

"Let's meet at the Dallas-Fort Worth Airport next Tuesday in the Southern Airlines lobby. We will fly to Houston, survey the area and pick the best spot for our action," Nix said. "There's a flight every other hour to Houston so I will meet you at 9:45 in the morning."

Tuesday morning Captain Nix and Billy Dean boarded the plane for the one and half hour flight to Houston. After landing they took a taxi to a local Rent A Wreck four miles from the airport. The 1998 Buick, with a small cracked windshield and dents on the front fender was just what the doctor ordered. They asked the office help where was the closes modest motel.

The attendant replied, "You mean the cheapest motel? That would be the Apache Motel over on El Paso Road. Go down two lights, turn right and you're on El Paso Road. The motel is about one mile south."

They checked into the motel, an infested one used by pimps and prostitutes. Several ladies with short shirts, net stockings, high heels and bright red lipstick, of the night, were walking up and down El Paso Road.

Early the next morning Nix and Dean entered the 98 Buick. Nix turned the key and watched black puffs of smoke bellow from the exhaust, filling the air. Nix gunned the car a couple times, then pulled out of the lot and headed downtown.

Finding a $5.00 a day parking lot, Nix pulled in and paid the attendant. They made their exit. Nix walked across the street while Dean continued to walk the side he was on merging at the end of the block,

"I don't see any possible way to do our business here at the Hotel. "Let's grab a bite to eat and go back to the motel. We will figure out what our next move will be." Nix said.

At the motel, Dean walked to the newspaper rack, just outside the front office of the motel, picking up the Houston Chronicle.

The headlines: Massive Manhunt for Killers.

Walking back to his room, Dean stopped for a moment, glancing through the article. A Federal Judge, a United States Senator from Nevada and a local Congresswoman from the Southside of Houston have been murdered. Dean opened the motel door and shoved the paper under Nix's nose. "Looks like we're ready to take back America," he said.

Both men sat on the edge of the bed, glancing through the paper, it showed pictures of the victims, FBI, CSI, and State and local police, looking for evidence, and pondered how they would fulfill their mission.

Dean smiled. "I remember the sniper kills in Iraq. You find a choice location, sit still and wait until the prey appears or you hide in a shelter area and pick your target off, one by one. It's a rush, checking the distance, scope and softly squeezing the trigger and watching the target hit the ground with a thud."

Captain Nix laughed.

"Here's an article about a Financial Convention in town. The main speaker is none other than our prey, Georg Staples.

Dean laughed. "When and where?" he asked.

"The Hilton Plaza Hotel on Airport Lane. That will be our best opportunity to take care of business. We need to drive to the Hilton and survey the place." Nix said.

In the afternoon they aimed their car to the Hilton. Captain Nix parked in the visitor slot, slid out and walked into the lobby of the Hotel. The lobby was huge, with an open café and bar at one end. There was a newsstand filled with magazines and large city newspapers, a ladies boutique, a cigar smoking room and soft chairs completed the interior.

Walking to the registration desk, Captain Nix inquired about the Convention. The lady behind the counter mentioned the luncheon was being planned in the Sam Houston Room. She pointed down the hall, the first door on the right.

"Thank you," Nix replied, tipping his hat.

He left the Hotel, and walked the short distance to the car, opening the door and slid in. "I'm still not sure this is the place or time," he said.

"Are they catering the luncheon or do they provide this on site?" Dean asked.

"As large as this operation is, I am sure they will do this on site. Why do you ask?"

"What if I was one of the staff serving lunch? We could go by a hardware store and pick up something that would make Staples extremely sick. So sick, they would have to take the old man to the hospital. We'd have a better chance at the hospital to complete this job," he said.

"Brilliant my boy, now how do you get hired?" asked Nix.

"Don't worry, leave that to me," he replied.

Dean walked through the service entrance at the back of the Hotel. Walking down the hallway, he opened the door to the employee's room and entered. Hanging on a rack were different sizes of white mid-range service jackets, shirts and black bow ties. Shuffling through the rack, he pulled one jacket, shirt and tie, and tried them on. As he stood before the mirror, he brushed his hand over the crew cut, "not bad at all," he laughed.

Before leaving, he took a couple towels, wrapped the clothing in them and walked outside. Smiling all the way to the car, he knew this caper would work. When he reached the car, he opened the door, threw the stuff on the back seat, and slid in the passenger seat. "Well, I am ready to be the server of Mr. Staples' demise on Thursday," grinning.

Thursday morning Nix drove to the service entry of the Hotel where Dean made his exit, picked up the clothes from the backseat and entered the building.

He was stopped by security.

"Are you the new help Temp Service sent over to help with the luncheon?" the security officer asked.

"Absolutely. Here's my outfit for the day. I just need to know where to hang my clothes until I am called to help serve," he said.

"The second door on the right, down the hallway," the security officer told him.

Dean walked down the hall, opened the door to find three Hispanic young men changing clothes. He smiled and said, "hello—(hola)." After changing clothes, the four walked to the kitchen area, joining the others that were waiting their assignment. As soon as he had his assignment; he started working alongside the other servers, placing tableware, cups and crystal glasses on the round tables.

Gazing at the exquisite décor, the Sam Houston Conference Room was decorated in brown tones and cream colored chairs surrounded the large over size tables, of dark brown wood. On the walls were pictures of Sam Houston, the Alamo and other Texan nobles. The head table was a large 6 x 10 table, lay with a white linen cloth underneath and a light brown overlay showing the heritage and history of Texas. The center two chairs were reserved for the President of the Conference and their major speaker, Georg Staples.

Dean took a mental picture of the scene.

In his mind, he figured how he would wait for the right moment, rush ahead of those lingering in the hallway and be serving the first roll of tables plus the head table with all the dignitaries.

His mind went blank for a split second.

He shook his head.

"Would it be the food, coffee or water?" he muttered to himself. "It will have to be the food. The coffee would taste bitter and the water would look cloudy," he finally concluded.

For a moment he was lost in time.

His mind carried him back to his college days, a time when he waited tables at Sir George's Smorgasbord. He shook his head to clear the image, which brought a smile, as he placed water pitchers on each assigned table.

Registration was over and the hall doors were open for the attendees to enter. Billy Dean stood at attention, dressed in a white jacket, white shirt and black bow tie, waiting for the attendees to be seated.

At the head table, the President and Speaker Staples shared laughs and small talk, while there was much chatter throughout the room.

The first speaker, John Davis, Senior VP Marketing for Chase, pointed to a powerpoint presentation on the screen. "Chase bank is proud to be a sponsor and endorser of Sharia Financing. Many of our foreign offices have been using this form of financing for a couple decades. Since it was instituted in America, many of our larger banking institutions have come on board. First, it is far different from America's banking regulation, yet, still offers an opportunity to make huge gains on our bottom line. Under Islamic Sharia Financing, interest or fees of money (riba or usury) is forbidden." He said, smiling.

Your question, as I read your facial expressions, "how do we make money if we do not charge interest?" Under Sharia Financing, Islamic rules on transactions have been created to prevent it. The basic principle of Islamic banking is based on risk-sharing which is a component of trade rather than risk-transfer which is seen in conventional banking. Islamic banking introduces concepts such as profit sharing (Mudharabah), safekeeping (Wadiah), joint venture (Musharakah), cost plus (Murabahah) and leasing (Ijar). He outlined some of the advantages of enlisting Sharia Finance as part of a bank or companies portfolio.

Davis paused, took a drink of water and continued. Using the pointer, he drew their attention to a couple examples. In an Islamic mortgage transaction, instead of lending the buyer the money to purchase the item, a bank might buy the item itself from the seller and resell it to the buyer at a profit, while allowing the buyer to pay the bank in installments. In order to protect itself against default, the bank asks for strict collateral. If there is a default, the bank sells the item and they split the proceeds or profit, according to their investment. Another way is Eljara wa Elqtina, which is similar to real estate leasing. Islamic banks handle loans for vehicles in a similar way (selling the vehicle at a higher than market price to the debtor and then retaining ownership of the vehicle until the loan is paid in full.

Davis laughed. "What do you think so far?"

Another innovative approach applied by some banks for home loans, called Musharaka al-Mutanaqisa allows for a floating rate in the form of rental. The bank and borrower form a partnership entity, both providing capital at an agreed percentage to purchase the property. The partnership entity then rents out the property to the borrower and charges rent. The bank and borrower will share the proceeds from this rent based on the current equity share of the partnerships. At the same time, the borrower in the partnership entity also buys the bank's share of the property at agreed installments until the full equity is transferred to the borrower and the partnership is ended. This method allows for floating rates according to the current market rate such as the BLR (base lending rate.)

Davis turned to the last slide. This is a powerful way to make money using Sharia Financing. This is a picture of a medium size corporation. This corporation called

XYZ needs funds to expand their business. Using the floating rate as our guide, we will be shareholders and our profit on the loan is equal to a certain percentage of the company's profit. Once the principal amount of the loan is repaid, this dissolves our profit sharing partnership.

In closing, another key component of Sharia Financing for any bank considering such; you will have a Sharia Supervisory Board, which gives you excellent advice and ensures that the operations and activities of the banking institution comply with Sharia principles.

Thank you and God bless the banking industry.

Davis received a standing ovation.

This brought a smile from Staples as he put his hands together, clapping for this venture.

It was now eleven fifteen and time for lunch.

Dean made his way to the head table, continued to pour water in empty glasses, turning he made his way to the kitchen. He carries out plates of food, placing them in front of the guest at the head table. Dean returned to the kitchen, picked up trays of food and carried them to other tables.

When the entire guest had been served, Dean turned to the side of the room, waiting for a motion of service. Standing straight as an arrow, arm raised slightly with a towel lay across it, watching intently at the head table. Lunch was over, except for a few stragglers finishing their Texas Pecan Pie, smothered with vanilla ice cream. President Billings stood to his feet, made a few remarks before introducing the esteemed guest of honor, Mr. Georg Staples.

There was a loud applause as Mr. Staples stood, walked to the podium and reached for the microphone. He raised his arms in a sign of victory.

Another great round of applause.

Ladies and gentleman, "it is my pleasure to address you today at this wonderful Global Financial Conference. I wish I had time to share with you how I made my billions, but I will save that for another day."

Suddenly, he bent over the podium, dropping the mike and fell to the floor. The President and many others gathered around him. Someone hollered call 911.

A doctor in the conference, approached and knelt down to check, "We must get him to a hospital now," he screamed at the top of his voice.

Shortly, the paramedics appeared and administer aid and then transported him to the nearest hospital facility.

Billy Dean snuck out through the kitchen and discarded his server outfit. He walked to the front of the Hotel waiting for a glimpse of Staples as they carried him out. Dean walked the few blocks to the $5.00 parking lot and met up with Captain Nix. They made their exit from the lot, following behind the ambulance, on its way to the hospital.

"Great job Billy," Nix said. "Tomorrow we will

call and check on his condition. Let's go and celebrate. I'm hungry for one of those famous Texas steaks."

BREAKING NEWS

Homeland Security has issued a complete lock-down of major cities — New York, DC, Chicago, Atlanta, Miami, Dallas-Fort Worth, Phoenix, Seattle, San Diego and Los Angeles. The assistant HLS, James Barnard issued the order by the way of the White House. There is a curfew on all outside activity after 10 p.m. The President will address the nation from the Rose Garden at 10 a.m. on Friday.

From the Rose Garden the President of the United States.

"American citizens, I have authorized the lockdown of our major cities for the protection of all Americans. We have been under a siege of assassinations of some of our most prominent members of Congress and business leaders across this great nation of ours. I have given the FBI the authority to use any and every means in apprehending these murderous radicals, including using the NSA monitoring cell phones and other means of communications. America will not be safe until they are brought to justice.

Thank you and God bless America."

"Mr. President. What do you think brought this on?" asked Jim Burns of the National Review. "Is it the Tea Party or other radicals like the Weatherman in the 60's?"

"That's a great question. I am not at liberty to answer that right now. I'll have to get back to you after I confer with my domestic intelligence team," he said. Raising his voice, *"and I don't appreciate you associating this group with the Weatherman."*

"Mr. President. You're doing a good job of running the country. Just one question; it appears there's more than one person, group or body involved in this, are you ready to prosecute all of them?" asked George Steinway of ABC News.

"Well George, let's catch them first. Someone out there in America has the information we need to put these mad men away."

"Mr. President. Are you willing to call out the National Guard or use some of our Stateside Army soldiers in this operation?" asked Charles Bolton of the Town Hall News Center.

"I am not sure it will come to that, but that is an option," the President said. *"That's all the time for questions. I have to get back to work. Thank you."*

EVENING NEWS:

It's 6 p.m. and all major networks are abuzz with the speech the President gave today. ABC, CBS, NBC and major stations in local areas were giving their spin on it.

"Are you safer today than you were four years ago?" was the question asked. "Our lines are open. We need you to call 800-243-1000 and give us your opinion?" The announcer said.

"Line one. You're on the air. What is your question?"

"Is this the start of martial law in America?" asked the caller.

"Well I wouldn't go that far. The President is only concerned with the safety of our citizens."

"You're on the air. What is your question?"

"Can you explain why I see Army soldiers, tanks, and Hummers on some of city streets, like in St. Louis?" the caller asked.

"To be honest, I haven't seen the video." the announcer said.

"You are on the air. What is your question?"

"Why is the President always apologizing to the Muslim world about our transgressions as the President stated in his Cairo speech?" the caller asked.

"Well, I wouldn't go that far. The President was only reaching out to the Muslim world with an olive branch. Telling the world we are not at war with Islam."

"You are on the air. What is your question?"

"Why is the President calling all these scandals phony?"

"That's a good question. I'll ask the President the next time I see him."

"You're on the air."

Chapter 17

St. Luke's Hospital

"This is Father Nix, St. Stephens Church. I am inquiring on the condition of Georg Staples."

The operator responded, "Father, I really can't give that information out. Why don't you try and talk with the hospital Chaplain. Let me ring his office."

"Thank you and God bless you," Nix said.

This is Chaplain Owens. How may I help you?"

"Chaplain Owens thanks for taking my call. This is Father Nix. I was inquiring about the status of Mr. Georg Staples. He was admitted to the hospital yesterday with some kind of bug."

"I haven't made my rounds this morning, but let me call the front office. I am going to place you on hold for a minute or two. . . "

"Father Nix, sorry it took longer than I thought. I understand that Mr. Staples is much improved this morning. They are going to keep him over the weekend. He is in a private room, 402."

"Thank you Chaplain. I will drop by and visit with him this afternoon. I have Mary Carter and Josie Gonzales in the same hospital. Maybe you could drop by their room and pray with them," Nix said.

In the background, Billy Dean barreled over laughing. When Nix got off the phone, Billy started in.

"Father Nix, Father Nix."

"Hey Billy, it's not funny. At least we know what floor and room Staples is in. Now we must figure out how to get to him in that room."

"There are only two chances. We either nail him in his hospital room, or when they bring him out in a wheel chair," Billy said. "Let's go by the hospital and check it out. Also, what's across the street from the entrance to the hospital?"

They entered the gas hog and headed toward St. Luke. When they arrived, Nix pulled into St. Luke's parking lot and both men slid out of the car. Dean walked around to the front entrance, while Captain Nix walked across the street. Turning to face the main entrance, the tall trees with their low lying branches hid the entrance.

At his back, he viewed the front of St. Luke Catholic Church. Walking around the corner to view the backside of the church, he rattled a couple doors, hoping to find an entrance inside. The next door, which led to the recreation hall, was open allowing Nix to peep inside. The room was filled with banquet size tables, chairs stacked against the wall and a wet bar in the corner. To his right was a stairway leading to the second floor. Making his way up the stairs, Nix entered a large room filled with boxes, bins and several white columns. A large window, on the east side of the room, let flickering rays of light in.

Walking to the window, he stumbled over a box, steadies himself and continued to the window. Pulling a hankie from his pocket, Nix rubbed the dirt and grime off, allowing an easy view of the hospital. He raised his arms, took sight of the entrance . . . bang, bang. "A perfect spot," he muttered.

Nix made his way out of the church and met up with Dean in the parking lot. "What did you find out?" asked Dean.

"It's a perfect spot to hit the target coming out of the hospital entrance," he said, "What did you find?"

"Each hospital wing is created in a circle. I don't see how we could get a good shot off," Dean told him.

Father Nix made a phone call the night before, acknowledging the release time that Mr. Staple would be dismissed from the hospital.

Daybreak broke the shadows coming through the blinds of their motel room. They jumped out of bed, freshened up and aimed the rental wreck to the hospital.

"I'm hungry. We have time for a bite to eat," Billy told Nix. "There's a small café up ahead."

They pulled into the parking lot of the Busy Bee Café, a tiny hole in the wall, which advertised genuine Texas food. As they entered the door, they could smell the aroma of bacon filling the air. The lady, standing behind the counter, smiled, "welcome" and motioned for them to take a table. They picked up the small menu, showing a large Cactus with a bee buzzing on a flower and gazed at the offerings. The waitress, with two glasses of water, strode to the table, laying the glasses on the table. She reached in her pocket and pulled out the order pad. "Are you ready to order?" she asked.

"What's in the garbage burrito?" Dean asked.

"Well, pausing, everything left over from dinner last night," laughing. All kidding aside, "you can have your choice of shredded beef, chicken, chorizo, sausage or bacon, with stir fried onions, tomatoes, potatoes, bell peppers, cheese and a splash of our famous salsa, wrapped in a large tortilla."

"Wow, guess we will have two garbage burritos, a side order of Texas toast and black coffee."

"Good choice," the waitress said.

Taking the last couple sips of coffee, "time to get on the road," Billy said.

Smiling at the pretty lady at the cashier desk, Billy told her how much they enjoyed the meal. She smiled and said, "thank you, come back and see us soon."

Walking out the door, Billy turned his head, taking another look at this beautiful . . . he stumbled. "Wow, if I didn't live so far away I'd be back in a flash."

Nix laughed. "Haven't you heard of long distance romance? The only problem they never seem to work out."

It was nine o'clock when they pulled in front of the Catholic Church. Captain Nix made his exit, carrying a small black case, and walked to the back of the church, while Billy drove around searching for a place to park.

Entering the back door Nix walked up the stairs to the open room. Pushing a couple crates aside, he placed the gun case down on one. While opening the case, his thoughts turned to a time in Vietnam . . . wiping his forehead and a tear that formed in the corner of his eye, he put the weapon together and walked to the window. Gazing across the street Nix picked out the best spot and angle to fire the weapon.

Dean was sitting in the lobby of the Hospital, waiting for the moment for Mr. Staples to be ushered out the door. He picked up several magazines and leafed through them quickly, still keeping his eyes on the door. .

Nix, still starring at the entrance, lifted the weapon up against his right shoulder, his left hand steady under the stock of the barrel, then focusing the sights until the beam crossed in a perfect square. All he had to do now was sit and wait. It was nearly eleven o'clock. Thoughts ran through his head, just who is this man, Georg Staples. He studied his life on Google and found so many things wrong, realizing he is not a patriot or a real lover of freedom and liberty. With all his wealth, he is a narcissistic human being. Guess the world won't miss much. Nix looked at his watch. It read ten-thirty.

"It won't be long now," he murmured to himself.

A black town car, with dark tinted windows,

moved slowly through the circle, coming to a stop in front of the double wide glass doors. The driver quickly made his exit. Walking to the other side, he waited for an orderly to push the patient out in a wheel chair. The double doors opened. The orderly pushed the wheelchair through the doors, locked the wheels, and helped the patient to stand. Standing, Staples smiled at the newsmen and photographers . . . .

Nix pushed the window open and lifted the weapon to his shoulder. Looking through the scope, he made a minor adjustment and squeezed the trigger. A blast, like the clap of thunder, filled the air. The target fell back against the webbing of the wheelchair. The orderly jumped back in shock, screaming at the top of his lungs. "Help, help, help." The driver of the town car, knelt down to help his boss . . . He screamed, "He's dead.

Chapter 18

Joe loaded his fishing gear in the back of the pickup, and aimed his vehicle to Ben's home. Arriving at 4 a.m., he walked on the wood porch, reaching down to pat Blue on the head and then knocked lightly on the back door. Ben opened the door and put his fingers to his lips . . quiet.

Stepping out the back door, Ben picked up his fishing gear, stepped off the porch and loaded it in the back of the pickup.

"We'll rent a boat from the marina," Ben said. Traveling on highway 33, dark clouds hid the moon, making the crooked two lane road dangerous. Joe slowly moved his pickup to the gravel, when a large dump truck barreled on his side of the road. "Whew, that was close," Joe said.

"The turn off to Cedar Grove is just ahead," Ben said. Turning left on the bumpy dirt road, the truck hit every pot hole, bouncing both boys in the air. "Hold on," Joe said. Rounding the bend in the dirt road, they could barely make out the flickering lights on the wood frame marina building. Joe slowed to a crawl, made a wide turn and stopped the truck. As they made their exit, they acknowledged a couple other fishermen leaving the building.

Picking from a display of boats on the wall, Joe picked and paid for a Tracker Grizzy aluminum boat with a Mercury 40HP motor. Leaving the marina shop, they picked up their gear from the truck and continued walking to the dock.

"This is it," Ben said. "What a way to spend a Saturday morning. Did your dad take you fishing?"

"Not really. My dad died when I was 7 years old. My grandparents raised me, after my mom remarried. Guess I missed a lot growing up," Joe said.

"I'm so sorry . "

"That's ok Ben . . . starting the motor. Splashing through the water, Joe opened the throttle, creating huge waves, hollered and asked, "Where to Ben?"

"There's a cove up ahead. This early in the morning, the fish should be hungry and ready to strike," Ben responded, as the boat sped through the blue/black water.

Slowing the boat to an idle, Joe maneuvered the boat some 40 feet from the bank, and shut off the motor.

"My dad always told me to sit still, let the sound of the motor subside. If there's a school of fish in the cove, we don't want to create a mini-tsunami," Ben said. Joe laughed.

Both men leaned back in the boat chairs, watching the floater bobble on top of the water. "Sometimes you catch fish, other times you just relax and enjoy . . . before Ben could finish, the float went under the water. Pulling up on the rod, Ben turned the reel, released the line, turned the reel again. Ten minutes later, the tug of war between man and fish was over. Joe lowered the net under the fish, lifting the 2 1/2 pound bass into the boat.

Joe reached in the tackle box, pulling out a fly and attaching it to the hook. He flipped the fly about thirty to forty feet, pulling the noisy buzz-bait across the surface. A prowling largemouth snagged the fly, down into the water the fly disappeared. Fighting . . . reeling . . . releasing . . . fighting . . . reeling . . . after a fight and struggle, Joe landed the biggest fish of the morning. "What a catch," Ben hollered.

The sun broke through the dark clouds for a brief moment or two and then hid behind heavy cumulonimbus clouds that darkened the heavens. Lightning flashed, followed by a large clap of thunder and heavy rain followed.

"I hadn't planned for this," Joe said. "We better head for shore." Reaching for the starter, he pushed it several times. "Heavens to Bessie, it won't start," he yelled at Ben.

"Let it sit a minute and then try it again," Ben told him.

"Come on baby, I'm getting wet, start." Joe pushed the starter again. Grinding a couple times, it turned, fired and started. Turning the boat, he aimed it back to the dock. When they reached the dock, they stepped out of the boat and high-tailed it to the truck.

"This won't last too long, they never do this early in the day," Ben said. "We still have a few more hours before dark."

Sitting in the truck, Joe asked, "I wonder what our next assignment will be? We are already making headlines on the major channels and the newspapers. There's a massive manhunt for these killers."

"Did you see the movie Bonnie and Clyde," Ben asked. "It was hilarious with the FBI chasing them from one bank job to another."

"Yes, I saw the movie, but they were caught in the end. Now I don't want to see that happen to us. Right!" Joe replied.

It stopped raining. The sun was shining through the floating gray clouds, and in the distance they could see a beautiful rainbow. Making their exit from the truck, they walked along the bank, splashing mud puddles and sliding on the slippery slope, until they came to a big rock.

"This should be a good place, especially with the tree stumps, so close to shore. There's usually catfish crawling along the bottom," Ben said.

Changing bait, Ben put a piece of chicken liver on the hook, while Joe placed three night crawlers. Tossing the line about ten feet in the water, Ben watched it sink to the lake floor. He slowly dragged the bait above the floor of the lake, watching for any movement in the line. A tug on his line caused excitement, reeling it in . . . an old shoe was attached.

Laughing, Joe yelled. "That's a great catch buddy."

Ben took the shoe off, throwing it back over his head in the bushes. He placed another liver on the hook; and cast the line in the water. Slowly dragging along the bottom he felt a tug on the line. Tightening the line, then slowly letting it loose. Again he tightened the line, working whatever was on the hook, slowly watching the water splash. He released the line, watching the fish move through the water, then dragged it in again, and finally reeling it close to shore, where Joe reached the net in under the fish, lifting it to shore.

"Look at that one," Ben said as he turned toward Joe. Guess it will weigh 6 pounds. We'll have catfish for Sunday dinner."

The setting sun cast a beautiful blazing red and orange hue to the sky, passing over the mountains. They picked up their tackle box, the fish box and walked back to the truck.

On the way home Ben quizzed Joe about Shirley.

"She's a looker and I understand she is a good Christian girl," Joe said, his face turning red. "She's alright I guess. I guess I need to go out with her."

"Why don't you get dressed up tomorrow, casual clothes is the norm at Sarah's church and go with us. Be here at 9 a.m. sharp. Sarah doesn't like being late.

Sunday morning Joe knocked on the door. Sonny ran through the house hollering "I'll get it." He opened the door and smiled at Joe. Opening the screen door, Joe walked into the living room. "Tell your dad I'm here."

"Well, well, look at you," Sarah said as she walked from the kitchen to greet Joe. "Quite handsome, if I say so myself. Shirley Jean is in for a shock."

"I hope it's not too big a shock," he replied.

"Are you staying for dinner? We will have some of the catfish you boys caught yesterday."

"I might if you twist my arm, besides that small apartment can be depressing at times."

"Would you mind if I invited Shirley Jean?"

Joe laughed. "They tell me the more the merrier, so I guess it's alright."

The morning worship was a day of celebration.

The worship team led the congregation in a blend of choruses: *Because He Lives, Come into His Presence, Holy, Holy, Holy, and How Great Thou Art.*

The pastor stood behind the pulpit, reading the 23rd Chapter of Psalms. "Today we are going to highlight just what the psalmist David meant in this Psalm. I want you to note the very first verse — *'The Lord is my Shepherd.'*

Notice the word *MY* which shows possession. So I can say The Lord is my Shepherd, my Savior, my Lord, my Healer, my Provider and my soon coming King."

Now David tells us *'I shall not want.'*

"This literally means I shall not want for anything I have need of that God wants me to have."

The pastor continued with this paraphrase of the

23rd Chapter of Psalms.

After the service concluded, Ben and his family and their guest, Joe Capps walked toward the exit. They shook hands with several people and Ben introduced Joe to several men.

Joe caught the eye of Shirley Jean, winked in a kidding way. Shirley's face turned crimson and her smile exposed the dimples in her cheeks. She was dressed in a blazing red skirt and vest contrasted with a long sleeve while satin blouse. The flow of her long blonde hair reached the middle of her back.

Walking between the pews; Joe stood beside her, smiled and asked, "are you coming over for dinner to-day?"

"Sarah invited me. So yes, I am coming over for dinner. I understand you and Ben caught the fish we are having," she replied. "Did you get caught in the thunder storm?"

"We got caught in the boat when torrents of rain began to fall. The motor wouldn't turn over, so there we were, two little boys getting soaked. Finally the motor turned and we made it to shore.

"May I walk you to your car or are you riding with Sarah?" Joe asked.

She turned and looked at her folks.

Dad shook his head up and down while Mom was busy visiting with another church couple.

"I'll ride with Sarah and meet you there?" she

whispered.

"Great. I'll meet you there."

Joe skipped a step or two on the way to his truck, murmuring, "I've never met a girl like Shirley."

Starry eyed, he bolted out of the church parking singing . . . on his way to Kroger's. He hopped out of the truck and ran inside the store, turning to his right and walked quickly to the cooler box holding various flowers. Standing in front of the flower box, he opened the door and picked out a beautiful vase with baby breathes and three red roses.

Chapter 19

WASHINGTON, DC
Democrat Party

The hallways of the United States Senate were buzzing with Senators and aids running from one office to the next. They were in a quandary of who will be elected to fill the chairmanship and speaker of the Senate, due to the death of their Nevada leader. Only two Senators have shown interest in pursuing the position, as many have backed off their staunch stand on immigration and Obamacare. Fear gripped the halls of Congress.

The President has assured both Houses that security measures are tight and he personally guaranteed their safety. The President called for the leaders of both parties to the White House to ascertain the next steps in selecting a leader, Immigration Reform and Obamacare.

"I want to address Congress tomorrow morning." the President said.

The next day, Congress convened and the appointed Speaker introduced the President of the United States. A great round of applause was heard from the Democrat side.

"Thank you, thank you, thank you," holding his arms up in victory. He addressed them in a solemn tone and paid tribute to the Senator from Nevada.

He continued, "I will decide what steps we are to take in combating this unruly mob, gang or revolution."

"Is that clear?" raising his voice.

"We will not operate this administration in the face of fear. If and when we locate them, we will use every means possible, including drones, to kill or disperse the enemy."

The President paused, then took a deep breath and continued, "Many of you are facing reelection this coming year. I want you to know that I stand with you in your concern, voting to continue the Affordable Care Act will be a hot topic during your campaign."

From the gallery of Congress came a reply, "you don't have to be reelected," heads turning in the democrat section to see who spoke.

"You are right Senator."

After his speech to Congress, the president walked to the Rose Garden to take questions from reporters that had anxiously been waiting.

He pointed at John, from the Washington Tribune.

"Thank you Mr. President. The whole country seems obsessed with Immigration and Obamacare, will you be able to salvage those for the future?"

"John, when I campaigned for this office, I assured the American citizens there would be hope and change. Change has come and we are still working on hope. Yes, this is part of my legacy and I am pushing hard to keep the lid on ACA or Obamacare, as you call it. Now, my thoughts on immigration. . . pausing . . . this will be the tricky one as those hardnosed Republicans want a secure border before even offering options on the table. I expect to have this legislation passed and on my desk for my signature before my second term is completed."

"Deborah, by the way you're sharp in that sleeveless blue dress." he said.

"Why thank you for the compliment Mr. President. I'll try and not be too tough on you today," she said.

This brought a chuckle from the reporters and even the President smiled.

"Why are our citizens so angry at Congress and you Mr. President? Can you explain what 'phony' means when you discuss the scandals that have cropped up in your administration?"

"I thought you were going to go easy on me," trying to smile.

"Look I've tried my best to work in a partisan way with both parties to get America back on track. I inherited a mess from the previous administration and with some good fortune we should come out on top. If Congress won't work with me, then I have no other recourse than to use the mighty pen and executive order."

He paused and took a deep breath.

"That's all the time I have for questions. My family is waiting for me to return. We are flying on Air Force One to our vacation destination."

The president turned and walked through the

double doors and out of sight.

There were mumbling among several of the reporters, but none ever brought up anything substantial to discuss.

As they were escorted out of the Rose Garden, one reporter started to ask a question, "isn't this a good time to go on vacation when we have a revolution going on and the Congressman and business leaders being killed?"

Before he could finish his question, another reporter nudged him in the side and softly spoke, "that's enough of that nonsense. If you want to continue to be invited back for briefings, you must not ever criticize this President.

Chapter 20

Million Man/Woman Rally
Independents, Tea Parties, Conservatives
Washington DC—Square

General William Boyd, Executive Vice President of Southern Media has called for a million man/woman march on Washington, DC to take back our country. His press release hitting many local news networks calls for change in the direction our country is going. The General mentioned the scandals that plague the White House, the coziness with the Muslim Brotherhood and our financial support of terrorist organizations.

"Did you hear that Ben? A million man/woman rallies in Washington," asked Joe. "We have a couple months to save the money for the trip. Do you think it is feasible for us to go?"

"I'm not sure I have the money. School is starting and you know what that means, clothes, shoes and school supplies for the twins," Ben said. "Why don't you go?"

"By the way did you call Shirley Jean about going to the movies Saturday with Sarah and me?" Ben asked.

"Not exactly, but I will get around to it before Saturday," Joe replied. "You are some piece of work, making that poor girl wait all week before you ask her to the movies. I am going to put you on the spot. You let me know by Wednesday evening. Hear me?"Ben scolded him.

Joe picked up the phone and dialed the number on the small piece of paper Shirley gave him. It rang three times. Joe hung up the phone. "What's the matter with me?" he muttered.

Walking outside, standing by a large oak tree, he mused of Sunday's events at church and the fish fry. Closing his eyes, images of Shirley in the red skirt, vest and white blouse appeared. Her eyes were huh, huh, blue or were they green. Whatever, they sparkled, and were so fitting with her long blonde hair. Kicking the dirt, he briskly walked back inside and picked up the phone. He looked at the number on the paper and dialed.

"Good morning."

"This is Joe Capps. May I please speak to Shirley Jean?"

"Just a minute," Mom said. Several minutes passed when Shirley's Mom picked up the phone. "She's busy right now. Are you the young man in church Sunday?" she asked.

"Yes ma'am. I am a friend of Ben and Sarah England."

Shirley ran into the room, to take the phone from her Mom. Mom pushed the disconnect button. "Young lady what is the meaning of this rude behavior?" Mom asked.

"Mom, I am 20 years old," Shirley barked.

"Joe is only 23. He works for himself and is taking

college courses on the internet, " tears flowing . . .

"Alright dear, let me talk with your dad when he comes in from work. Whatever he decides, that is final." Mom told her.

Shirley ran to her room, shutting the door with a bang and lay across the bed and . . . . .

As soon as Shirley's Dad walked through the door, Mom motioned for him to come to the kitchen. Tossing his briefcase on the sofa, he walked to the kitchen.

"Ok honey, what's wrong now?" he asked.

"Your daughter has been locked in her bedroom all afternoon. She had a call from the young man she met at church Sunday. I wouldn't let her talk to him until you came home."

Dad poured a cup of coffee and sat down at the kitchen table. Now, pausing, 'let's go over this again. You wouldn't let her talk to this young man. Let's put it in perspective. Shirley is a wonderful daughter. She has a good head on her and she is 20 years old."

"I know all of that," Mom said.

"Then what's the problem?" He growled.

Dad finished his coffee and walked to Shirley's door, tapping a couple times. "Shirley, its Dad. I need you to come out and talk with us. Shirley its Dad."

Shirley rose from the bed. "I'll be out in a few minutes Dad. Let me freshen up first." After washing her face and brushing her hair, she closed the door and walked to the kitchen. Standing in the doorway, she . . . . .

"Honey, you're a wonderful daughter and your Mom and I are really proud of you. Why don't you call Sarah England and have Sarah tell Joe to give you another call?" Dad said.

After dinner, Shirley walked to the living room, picking up the phone, she called Sarah. "Shirley explained what happened when Joe called."

Sarah laughed. "You're 20 years old and they did what?"

Shirley Jean laughs. "It is ridicously funny now that I think of it. Quite embarrassing too. Will you call Joe and have him call me again. I promise to answer his call?"

Chapter 21

The next morning Ben drove to the Post Office to check his mail. Pulling the mail out of the box, a brown envelope was in the mix, without any return or identification. Walking to a table nearby, he leafs through the mail, throwing the junk and advertisements in the trash container. Leaving the Post Office, with the brown envelope in his hand, he proceeds to open the door of his car and drive to the City Park. .

"I wonder what this assignment is," he muttered, picking up the envelope, and then sliding out from behind the wheel. Walking toward the picnic table, Ben rips it open and lets the CD slide out. Noticing the paper, lodged in the envelope, he tore the envelope back, revealing one half of a woman's head. Joe must have the other half of the puzzle. Thinking, "I have to go out of town next week. That would be a good time to take care of business."

Scanning the area, there were several mothers, watching their small children play on the swings, whirl-a-bird, and in the sandbox. He smiled, thinking of the times Sarah had brought the twins to the park. Smiling at the little girl on skates, he waved at several of the mothers, as he continued walking to his car.

A voice behind him hollered, "Mr. England, Mr. England."

Turning around, he came face to face with a young woman. "Hi. My name is Julie Anderson. Your children are in my Sunday School Class. I just wanted to tell you how well behaved they are."

"Why—huh, thank you. That's very kind of you. I'll tell Sarah when I get home. What's your name again?"

"Julie Anderson," she said. "Have a nice day."

"Thank you. I'll be sure and let Sarah know. She'll be pleased to hear that."

Entering the car, he slid under the wheel, opened a notebook that lay on the front seat and scribbled Julie Anderson. Ben looked around; his gaze took in everything, the mothers, children, play sets and the two men, in business attire, walking by his car. He paused, watching the men walk further down the path, before placing the CD in the slot. There was a slight pause . . . then the voice of a woman, "Your mission will take you to Chicago. A leader in this administration will be attending the funeral of a loved one. She has the ear and heart of the President and her advice has been detrimental to our cause of freedom and liberty. You will learn more on line. Her name is Val. As soon as you hit the eject button, the CD will eject and slowly dissolve."

Pulling out of the park, Ben aimed his car in the direction of the office. When he arrived, he made his exit, picking up his briefcase and walked through the reception area and continued to his office.

Once inside, Ben picked up a gun manufacturing

magazine laying on his desk and wrote down the name of the largest gun manufacture in Chicago, Mid-West Gun Manufacturing Company. Scanning through the article, he noticed the company will move to another state in the near future. "This will be a great cover and a good time to take care of business."

After dinner, Ben retired to the living room, while Sarah and the twins cleaned the table and washed the dishes. He turned on WTOD, his favorite news channel.

A SPECIAL REPORT

"Another top official in this administration has been assassinated. From reports coming in from the field, yet not confirmed, it is the Sharia Czar Mohammad Elihu. Facts are slow coming in, but we'll have a full report at eleven.

Ben picked up the phone and called Joe.

When Joe answered there was a brief pause, "hello, this is Joe."

"Hey Buddy, did you get any merchandize in the mail? I received a package today. Why don't you come over for dinner tomorrow night. Wait a minute, let me check with Sarah."

"I'm back. She said ok, but she was going to invite Shirley Jean. How about six thirty?"

The Next Night

Joe arrived a little early and knocked on the door. Sonny ran through the house hollering "I'll get it." Sonny opened the door and greeted Mr. Joe with a grin. "There's a girl in the kitchen," giggling, pointing toward the kitchen. Running ahead of Joe to the kitchen, Sonny pulls at Shirley's skirt, "Shirley, Shirley, Mr. Joe's in the living room," grinning.

Walking into the living room, Shirley smiled, "welcome, it's nice of you to come." Joe smiled, putting his fingers to his lips. He pulled a bouquet of flowers from his back, telling her, "these are for Sarah." Walking to the kitchen, they stood in the doorway, watching Sarah pull a pan of biscuits from the oven.

"Everything smells so good," Joe said. Pulling the bouquet from behind his back, "These are for you Sarah."

"Joe, you didn't have to. They are beautiful. Thank you. Here Shirley, hold them while I get a vase."

She reached on the top shelf and picked a crystal glass vase. After pouring water in the vase, she carried the flowers and placed them on the buffet.

"Shirley and I are going to fix a peach cobbler for dessert, so all of you scoot."

This suited Ben and Joe, as they retired to the front porch, and sat in the white wicker chairs. The twins ran out the front door, yelling at the top of their lungs, and headed for the swing set.

"Ok Joe, what did you receive?" Ben asked.

Joe pulled a cream colored envelope from his

jacket. "It says our business is in Chicago. The woman's last name is Jacobs. Are we a match?"

"Right on. I'll call on the Gun Manufacturing for business and we can survey the area around the funeral home. Ms. Jacobs will be in the city to attend a relative's funeral. Timing is critical."

"Sorry to break up your little huddle fellows, but the peach cobbler is hot and ready," Sarah said.

Ben yelled for the twins to come in, opening the screen door to let Joe walk in first. They strode to the kitchen, picked up an enamel bowl of peach cobbler and vanilla ice cream and departed to the living room.

During their conversation, Ben mentioned the trip to Chicago. A large gun manufacturing company will be moving out of state and I need to test the waters for future orders.

Joe finished the cobbler. "Wow that was great Sarah."

"There more in the kitchen. Let me have your bowl."

"If you insist, you won't have to twist my arm twice."

"Shirley was a big help in the kitchen. In fact, she mentioned that she had a special recipe for stuffed pork chops. I laughed at her, a special recipe. She said she would cook them next week if you are here to taste the goodies."

Ben laughed. "Like they always say, the way to man's heart is through his stomach or something like that."

They laughed and laughed. So hard, Shirley's eyes swelled with moisture. Wiping the tears, she said, "let me help with the dished before I leave. I have to be at work early in the morning."

Joe stood to his feet, stuttered for a moment, then asked, "May I drive you home?"

She replied, "it would be a pleasure to ride in your truck."

Chapter 22

Chicago

Monday morning, Ben and Joe loaded the vehicle with two suitcases along with their two small black cases in the trunk. Walking back into the house, Sarah poured two cups of coffee and lay them on the kitchen table.

"Guess this will be an expensive trip," Joe said.

"I just need to be careful and keep a good account of what I spend." Ben said.

"May I use the telephone?" Joe asked.

"Of course, help yourself. Bet you are going to call Shirley Jean."

Pulling a paper from his billfold, he read the number aloud, before dialing. "Just a minute please, while I locate her?" the receptionist said.

"This is Shirley, how may I help you?" she asked.

"This is Joe Capps speaking. Is this the Shirley Jean I remember wearing a red shirt, vest and white blouse in church recently?" he asked.

"Yes Joe, this is the one and only. What's on your mind so early this morning?"

"Ben and I are going to Chicago on business and I wanted to know if you will miss me."

In the background, Ben was laughing, and choked

on the coffee . . .

"Of course I will miss you. Gotta go now. Bye."

Walking out to the car, Sarah waited for Ben to open the door. He turned, smiling at his beautiful wife, embraced her, softly kissing . . . then hearing her whisper, "be careful."

It would be 40 to 50 minutes before they would hit the interstate heading northeast to Chicago. As they traveled, Joe reached over and turned the radio on. A country hit by Billie Rae Cyrus was booming from the speakers in back. Singing with the music, "I hope Shirley Jean doesn't break my achy, achy breakey heart."

Turning his head Ben laughed, "You sure have a bad case of it now." They both laugh.

"Do you remember the million man/woman march coming up?" Ben asked. "I was thinking that General Boyd looked a lot like General Robert Lee. Do you think they are one and the same?"

"Come to think of it, they do have some of the same features and their mannerism is similar," Joe responded. "It appears we have camps all over the South, and we are getting ready to take back our country, to its roots of self-government, liberty and freedom."

Cruising on I-75, they marveled at the rolling hills and the beautiful bluegrass region of Kentucky. Traveling through Lexington they could see mile after mile of white fences and horses running loose in the lush velvet Bluegrass. In the distance, southern style homes radiated their charm with an invitation to come and sit a spell.

"Why do they call the grass blue or Bluegrass?" Joe asked.

"I'm not sure. I read somewhere it's called a smooth meadow grass, that when the plant is allowed to grow to its natural height, the flower heads are blue.

"Why here and not someplace else?" Joe asked.

"I understand breeders, that monitored their horses, found those that grazed in the Bluegrass Region appeared more hardier than those of other regions. Some breeders had the soil tested and found high calcium . . . maybe that's the answer. And don't forget, we have Churchill Downs," Ben said.

Joe laughed, "so in a nutshell, we live in the Bluegrass State of Kentucky."

Passing the last white fence, Joe said, "it is beautiful, but I still like the mountains and the Tri-State area."

"Have you ever wondered why we have three different dialects? Central Kentucky has a certain sound and then closer to the big cities . . . Louisville, Lexington and Covington, seem to be a little more sophisticated. Then on the tip of Kentucky, Tennessee and Virginia, we have a certain slow pace and drawl?" asked Joe.

Ben laughed. "Guess you could take voice lessons and get rid of the Southern drawl."

"Nooooo thank you. I guess I will stay with what I have," Joe replied.

Crossing the Ohio River Bridge between Kentucky

and Ohio, they entered Cincinnati, Ohio. Cincinnati is home to two major sports teams, the Reds baseball and the Bengals football. Cincinnati is often referred to as "Paris of America," for its well known historic architecture: Music Hall, Cincinnatian Hotel and Shillito Department Store.

"What is your favorite baseball team?" Ben asked. "I like the Braves, but the Reds have a rich history. I remember reading about the big Red Machine," Joe said.

"I need to stop and get some gas. While we're at it, why not stop and eat. I understand Cincy is well known for their spaghetti covered with chili." Ben said.

"I love chili, chili dogs with all the works, but whoever heard of chili over spaghetti. It will be a new experience for me," Joe replied.

They pulled off I-75, onto a side street that advertised fast food. Stopping at a Gulf gas station, Ben slid from under the wheel, and filled the tank. When he strode inside to pay the attendant, he asked, "Where they could get some of Cincinnati's famous spaghetti and chili.

The attendant told him to stay on this road. About a mile from here you will find the Cozy In Café. They'll have what you want and plenty of it. A little further down the road you will see the sign, I-75. "Where you boys headed?" the attendant asked.

"We're heading to Chicago to see about a job," Joe blurted out. "Not much work where we live."

Entering the Cozy In Café, they waited for a waitress to address them. The country theme of the café, chrome tables covered with red and white check oil cloth, chrome chairs with vinyl red cushions and one end of the dining area, stood an old juke box, out of the 50's. The place was loud and noisy and most of the tables were filled with patrons eating lunch, so they decided to sit at the lunch counter. The waitress squeezed by another waitress, handed them a menu and said, "Be right back," as she moved down the counter with the coffee pot. The menu had regular fare for a café; hamburgers, hot dogs, a variety of sandwiches, but outstanding was a picture of spaghetti piled high with chili, cheese and onions. "Guess we don't have to look any further," Ben smiled.

"Hi boys, I see you are smiling at the big plate of spaghetti. Sorry to disappoint you but we're sold out," the waitress told them.

"Sold out! What kind of a place is this . . . advertising Cincinnati Chili and you're sold out," Joe replied. She smiled real big, "gotcha." Two orders of world famous Cincinnati Chili coming up. "Now what would you like to drink? Two RC Cola's coming up."

After cleaning their plates, they ordered a piece of pecan pie with vanilla ice cream to finish off the meal.

"Fellows, was that satisfying?" she asked, laying the bill on the counter.

"Yes ma'am. It was so good, I will get my wife to try and match it when I get home," Ben said. He pulled out a five for the tip, placing it on the counter and then walked to the cashier to pay the bill.

"Thank you gentleman, trust everything was to your satisfaction," she said, as they opened the door. Joe turned his head, "it was excellent . . . first time I ever had spaghetti covered with chili.

Back on the road again, they came to the dividing section of I-75 to Detroit and I-72 North to Chicago, the last leg of their journey. "I'm tired," Ben said. "Why don't we turn in for the night?" The sign up ahead mentioned; restaurants, motels and rest stop. Ben made the exit, taking the side road to the Holiday Express. Pulling in front of the Hotel, they slid out and made their way through the lobby to register for the night.

Early the next morning, the sun's rays beamed through the blinds, arousing Joe. He slid out of bed, and strode to the bathroom. Walking out of the room, he punched Ben, sleeping in the other double bed. "Time to rise and shine, we have a big day ahead of us."

Ben crawled out of the sack. Stretching his frame, he put one foot in front of the other, making it to the bathroom. Several minutes passed . . . Ben was still running the water in the shower.

Joe knocked on the door, "Come on Ben. It's getting late."

"Let me finish . . . " he hollered, "I'll be out in 10." Ben finally opened the door, dressed in jeans and a plaid sports shirt. "I'm ready to eat," he said.

They locked the door, strode down the hallway and entered the elevator to the lobby. When the door opened, the aroma of bacon was too much. Staring at the buffet, loaded with breakfast goodies, Ben filled his plate with biscuits, gravy, bacon and eggs. Meanwhile, Joe settled for scrambled eggs, toast and fruit.

"Not like home, but what can you expect up north," Ben said, finishing the last few bites.

"Almost time to hit the road," Joe said.

"One more stop. Upstairs for me, I have some unfinished business to attend too."

Joe slid under the wheel, while Ben stretched out, laying his head back against the headrest. "It's less than a four hour trip, we should have plenty of time to decide where, how and when to strike," Ben said.

Cruising along at top speed . . . time flew by.

Joe noticed several signs indicating they were approaching the city limits of Chicago, when suddenly he pushed the brake pedal, slowing to 35mph. The midmorning traffic heading downtown slowed to a crawl.

"Wow I wasn't expecting all of this," he said.

"Welcome to the Big Windy City," Ben said. Laughing, "What did you expect? Remember we are not at home, so keep your eyes on the road and leave space between you and the auto in front of you."

"What do you know about heavy traffic?" Joe asked.

"One time I was on the 25E Express, going to Knoxville, laughing . . . that was a joke . . . 25E Express.

"Do we look for a hotel this early in the day?" Joe asked.

"We won't be able to get a room until after three this afternoon, so let's drive by the mortuary and stake it out. The turn off should be a couple miles ahead. We can take the side streets to Drake's Funeral Home."

Chapter 23

White House
Conference Room

The President called his security team together; Department of Justice, Secretary of State, Home Land Security, Department of Defense and the Federal Bureau of Investigation.

Pounding on the table, "this has gone far enough. I want some answers and I want them now. I am the President and no one, not the Tea Parties, Conservatives, Bible thumbing Christians or anyone else will stand in my way. Do I make myself clear?"

"Mr. DOJ, give me the scoop of what your department is doing to eradicate this problem?" he demanded.

"Well, pausing, Mr. President, uhhh, we are doing our best to find the culprits killing our leaders," bowing his head in shame.

"Not good enough. I want every Assistant Attorney General on this case. I don't want to hear any more excuses. You hear me," the President's voice became louder and louder.

"We have lost our Home Land Security Director to this group. She was a valuable member of our team and now she is dead. Someone knows what is going on. We may have to call on the American citizens for help."

Mr. Assistant HLS. "What are you doing about the security of our people? This is embarrassing. We can't keep our staff safe. Give me some answers? And don't heehaw with some dumb excuse why we don't know who these citizen terrorist are."

"Mr. President. They have been hitting in so many different places it is hard to pin point just who or what organization is in charge. We have hundreds of foot soldiers on the streets now. Sir we are giving it our best shot."

His eyes were ablaze, like a red hot poker. He yelled, "Your best shot isn't good enough. This makes me look weak in the eyes of the public. Contact NSA and see what they have. They have been monitoring domestic calls and emails. There has to be a leak some place and I want it now," he shot back at the director.

Steaming from all the wrong answers, the President took off his coat, rolled up his sleeves and shot imaginary hoops, one after another. Finally, winding down, he made one last ditch effort to get his team on the same page.

"Madam Secretary, I want you to work close with the CIA to see if there are any foreign agents in our midst. I don't think it is the Muslims so leave them out of the loop," he told her.

"Mr. FBI director, this should fall right up your alley, so I want every possible agent on this pronto. You will work closely with HLS and each hand will know what the other hand is doing."

Turning to the DOD Director, "I want you to think about calling out the National Guard. I will give you my command if it warrants this action."

"Are we all on the same page," he asked. "Let's get the job done and no ifs, ands or buts. I want results."

The President took a deep breath . . . "I need to see the Home Land Security and AG Director. The rest of you are excused," he told them.

"Eric I am putting my faith and trust in you to get this under control. If we lose this battle, everything both of us have worked so hard, changing America into a system that will eliminate much of the Constitution. Do you remember one of the Supreme Court Judges telling a group in South Africa that she wasn't pleased with our old Constitution and would not recommend or endorse it for any other country? She's the type of person we want on our side. The change is coming . . . as I promised the American people."

"Thank you for your help," Joe said.

Entering the car, Joe pointed to the map and directions to the cemetery. "Let's go and check it out." he said. Pulling from the parking lot, Ben aimed the car toward the cemetery. Driving slow on the two lane highway, they approached a beautiful scroll metal fence, enclosing rolling hills of Evergreen. The sign on the highway, showed one mile to the entrance to the cemetery. Turning right off the highway, the tree lined road led to the entrance. Scrolled, exquisite artistic lettering, Evergreen Cemetery, arched from one large white wrought iron column to the other.

Joe slowly moved through the cemetery, stopping at the burial plot shown on the map. Looking over the surroundings, he noticed a small knoll with several small trees west of the site. "That could be the spot we are looking for," He said.

They drove slowly around the area, stopping near the knoll. Joe and Ben made their exit from the car and walked fifty feet or so to the top of the knoll. Both men took turns looking through the small trees, raising their arms up in a shooting position at the grave site. Ben shook his head. "This is the best spot. Now we need to check her out at the funeral home. We need to see what she is wearing and be sure she is our target."

Early Wednesday morning they stopped at a fast food place and purchased two sausage/egg sandwiches and coffee to go.

Chapter 24

Drake Funeral Home
Chicago, Illinois

Driving slowly down the street, Joe passed the Funeral Home. It was a large white frame building with two large pillars on the front entrance. Parking on a side street, both men made their exit, walking along the left side of the building. On the back lot, to the left of the parking area was a crematory. This could give them an advantage, but not during daylight hours. Across the street were several small businesses and a vacant house. They walked across the street, surveyed the vacant house from various angles. Again, this would be hard to accomplish their mission during the day.

"Let's drive out to the grave site," Joe said. "I'll go inside and inquire the time of service and location of the cemetery." Opening the door, Joe stepped inside, and noticed the office to his right. A lady stepped out of the office and introduced herself. "I just arrived in town and need information on the Jacobs funeral and the directions to the cemetery?" Joe told her.

She handed him a map, showing the directions the funeral car would take to the cemetery. "It was approximately four miles from here."

When they reached the Funeral Home, Ben parked around the corner where the hearse would be stationed. They had an optimum view of the parking lot and watched each automobile enter the lot. A black Lincoln sedan, with government plates pulled in and parked. The driver quickly made his exit, moving to the passenger side and opened the back door to let a woman exit. She was dressed in a black pants suit with a white blouse that puffed around her neck.

Joe lowered his head and mentioned to Ben, "That's our target." They slowly moved from the parking spot and made their way to the cemetery.

When they arrived at the cemetery, Ben made the turn onto the tree lined road to a security post and waved at the attendant. Moving slowly around the bend, Ben pulled under a shade tree, waiting for the procession to arrive. Opening the trunk, Joe pulled out the small black case. He placed the case on the back seat and put the weapon together, lifted it to his shoulder, adjusting the scope. "I'm ready for action."

The procession moved slowly through the cemetery to the grave site. The casket was removed from the hearse and the pallbearers moved in step to the grave site. Standing at the head of the casket, the minister invited the family to be seated on the front row. After a short devotion, he closed with a prayer of peace, love and comfort from God the Father, the Son and the Holy Spirit. The minister asked those that had a rose to come forth and place it on the casket.

Joe stationed himself, looking through the small trees, he knelt to one knee. Steady . . . raising the weapon to his shoulder, he focused the scope a minuet degree. The target rose from her chair and placed the single rose on the casket. A single shot whizzed through the air, striking the target. She leaned over the casket then fell to the ground. Panic . . . . mourners screamed, running for cover.

Joe paused for a moment to view the reaction. Some rushed to the body while one gentleman knelt down and tried CPR. He looked up. "It's no use," he said. "She's gone."

Joe walked slowly back to the car, placed the weapon in the black case and shoved it in the trunk before entering the passenger door. Ben moved slowly toward the exit, on the opposite side of the cemetery, and headed back to the Interstate.

Chapter 25

Tallahassee , Florida
CAIR and the Rule of Law

CAIR—Council of American Islamic Relations with state headquarters in Tampa announced Muslim Day at the Capitol. Muslims will invade the Capitol on September 6, in order to present their case of racism and bigotry, with the intentions of influencing lawmakers on the benefits of Muslims in America. Adwar Buhle, the executive director of CAIR will be speaking on the steps in front of the Capitol.

Southern Media, under the leadership of retired General Boyd, indicated that thousands of patriots will invade Tallahassee to counteract CAIR's endeavors, during their Muslim Day at the Capitol. "We will fight fire with fire," he stated.

Captain William Nix and Billy Dean received their next assignment. Stopping at a local coffee shop, they swapped notes and details, while downing a cup of flavored coffee.

"It looks like our assignment will take us to the heart of the countries power struggle, Washington DC. There's going to be a million Muslim march on September 11. Our target will be sent in the next package," Nix told him.

"That's a couple weeks away. What do we do in the meantime?" Billy asked.

"We will sit tight until we receive orders to move out," Nix said.

September 6:

Hundreds of people gathered on the Capitol steps for this important rally, opposing Muslim Day March on the Capitol. Southern Media's foot soldiers, wearing red and white flag shirts with a blue background and white stars, were passing out copies of the Constitution. Many leaders made headway to the halls of the Capitol building, talking with legislatures, sharing the Constitution booklet and other pamphlets outlining the difference between Sharia Law and our Constitution.

CAIR director, Adwar Buhle stood on the steps in front of the Capitol building, addressing the Muslim followers. He shared about the great benefits American Muslims have been to the great State of Florida and America.

"We are indeed true Muslims adhering to the tenets of our faith, Islam," he said.

Shouts of praise, "be upon Allah" came from the crowd. He continued with more of the same, with the fervor and passion of a country evangelist, more shouts of praise "be upon Allah."

General Boyd, walking up the steps, smiled at the CAIR director. Standing side by side, General Boyd pulled a Constitution book from his jacket, showing it to the crowd of patriots and Muslims.

"This is a copy of America's Constitution," he told them. "Now I would like to compare notes and features of our Constitution and what the CAIR director, Mr. Buhle tells you about Sharia. In his previous speeches he advocated that Sharia is compatible with our Constitution. I am going to read from the Constitution and let the director tell us in his own words the difference if any."

"First of all I would like to make this statement, so that the press and our politicians will have a full understanding of what we, Southern Media believe. We are not anti-Muslim. We are anti-Islam. Islam's components consist of; religion, political, military, economic, and social ideology that are absolutely anti-American and our Constitution. *Muslims are people, not a race, who adhere to the tenets of Islam.* Many of them are ignorant of what Islam actually teaches. Therefore it is entirely possible to be anti-Islam without being anti-Muslim. We are such people."

"Our first amendment reads:

The First Amendment to the U.S. Constitution states that Congress shall make no law prohibiting the free exercise of religion, shall not abridge the freedom of speech, the right of the people to peaceably assemble and Congress cannot take away the right of the people to petition the Government for the redress of grievances.

"Mr. Buhle, will you please address how Sharia is

compatible with our Constitution?" asked the General.

His face turned crimson, small beads of sweat appeared on his forehead. He stuttered for a moment. "Well, I want you and all these here to know that Islam is a religion of peace."

"Sir I didn't ask you if Islam was a religion of peace. We are here at the Capitol debating how and why our politicians should even entertain Sharia or any foreign or international law in conjunction with our Constitution. Now will you answer the question?" Boyd asked him.

There was uproar among the Muslim group standing on the steps and the sidewalk. Shouting profanities and Allah is great, trying to drown out the General.

Director Buhle, turning from the crowd, ran up the steps to the entrance of the Capitol. He opened the door and vanished out of sight. Many of his followers dispersed, walking toward the entrance.

General Boyd, reading from the pamphlet, "let me enlighten you to the difference between the Constitution and what CAIR has to offer under Sharia. Listen to what Mohammad the prophet had to say about his religion:

1. "Whoever changes his religion kill him."

2. Islamic law barred them from observing their practices and relegates non-Muslims to 'dhimmi' status, where they are not to propagate their customs amongst Muslims and cannot display a Cross or the Star of David or abridge 'the freedom of speech.'

1. Islamic law enforces dhimmi status on non-Muslims prohibiting them from observing their religious practices publicly, raising their voices during prayer, ringing church bells or say anything considered 'insulting to Islam.'

The First states Congress cannot take away "the right of people to peaceably assemble."
1. Islamic law states that non-Muslims cannot repair places of worship or build new ones, they must allow Muslims to participate in their private meetings, they cannot bring their dead near the graveyards of Muslims or mourn their dead loudly. Islam prohibits them from observing their religious practices publicly, raising their voices during prayer, ringing church bells or say anything considered 'insulting to Islam.'

The First states the Congress cannot take away the right of the people "to petition the government for a redress of grievances."
1. Islamic law states non-Muslims are not to harbor any hostility toward the Islamic state or give comfort to those who disagree Islamic government.
The Second Amendment states "the right of the people to keep and bear arms shall not be in-

fringed."
1. Islamic law states that non-Muslims cannot possess arms, swords or weapons of any kind.

General Boyd ended his presentation.

"There's more than what we have time for, but I think you get the jest of what Islam's Sharia is all about. It is a system that controls every aspect of your life, political, military, religious and social. Now let's go inside and visit with our local politicians. We have a war to fight and we will be victorious if we are all on the same page."

The General turned and walked along with all of his supporters, toward the double doors that opened to the Capitol building.

Chapter 26

Washington DC
September 11, 2014

Captain William Nix and his side kick, Billy Dean boarded American Blue Airlines heading for Dulles International Airport. Captain Nix sat about middle ways of the plane while Dean was several rows back. As they departed, both men smiled at each other and made their way to the baggage department. Nix shuffled his black briefcase to his right hand. Standing near the baggage rack, he watched suitcases turn the curve and finally pulled his lone blue suitcase off the rack. Clutching the briefcase under his arm, he pulled the suitcase toward the Spend-Thrift Auto Rental. Dean was still standing at the carrousel waiting for his luggage to appear. Finally, the black suitcase with the blue handle appeared. He picked it up and strode toward the car rental. Standing in the shadows, Dean waited until Nix was ushered outside to pick up the rental.

Walking several feet behind, Dean waited until Nix entered the car before stepping off the curb. He continued to walk between two rolls of cars before opening the backdoor to place his luggage on the seat.

"Guess we are in the big time now," Dean said.

"Arrangements have been made for us to stay a couple days at a motel, on the outskirts of the airport. I'm not familiar with this airport so look for the exit sign that will allow us to leave," Nix said.

"Get in the right lane, the exit to Airport Road is just ahead. This should take us to Main Street and a short hop to the motel," Dean said.

A large sign pointing to the Airport Motel was just ahead. Nix pulled into the entrance lane and both officers made their exit, walking to the small office to register.

The attendant gave Nix the key to room 107. "Gentleman it is close to the left end of the motel. There's an ice machine in the middle of the complex. Have a nice stay," he told them. "Oh, I almost forgot. There's a package here for Nix.

Nix picked up the package. Once inside the motel room, he closed the blinds and turned on the table lamp, before opening the package. Nix smiled, pulling his special weapon from the box. A note was attached to the trigger, identifying the next target. "We have a big one this time Billy."

"Let me see?" Dean asked.

Nix handed the information to him, waiting for a reply. "Why, I thought it would be one of CAIR's big wigs and the Million Muslim March. It's the CIA director. I understand he converted to Islam a long time ago. Makes one wonder why the president would put someone with such a varied radical background in charge of the CIA," Dean stated.

"If it's the same to you Billy, we might want to kill two birds while we are in DC.

"General Boyd mentioned that our contact in Washington would be of help. I have a secret code and number to contact him. He's a real patriot and despises what is happening to our country."

"Let's go out and find something to eat?" Dean said. "I'm starved." They placed the black cases in the trunk of the car and left the motel. "What are you hungry for?" asked Nix.

"A juicy hamburger, fries and a chocolate milk shake." Dean said.

"On the way to the motel I noticed a nice looking hamburger stand not far from here. Let's check it out," Nix said. They parked the car and entered a 50's diner . . . with all the posters of the early 50's hanging on the wall. There was a picture of Marilyn with her white dress blowing in the wind, a picture of James Dean, Rebel without a Cause and the Rat Pack, Frank, Sammy and Dean plus others.

"Billy, you are too young to remember all of these," smiling as he related the story of each poster. They sat at the soda fountain counter and picked up a menu— simple deluxe hamburgers, cheese burgers and some with different condiments. Billy ordered two deluxe hamburgers, French fries and a chocolate shake. Captain Nix order a deluxe hamburger topped with pickles, tomato, lettuce and a mixture of pickled peppers and black coffee.

"Wow, this is about as good as it gets," Billy said. He ordered another side of French fries. After finishing their meal, they stopped and looked at the pictures on the wall again. On the way to the motel, Nix stopped at a convenience store and picked up the local and DC paper.

"What are you looking for in the papers?" asked Billy.

"Well you never know what you will find, especially in the DC paper. They have a ton of political news and events. This may give us a clue of where, when and how to take care of business."

"Man, you've been at this a long time. I wouldn't have thought of that in a thousand years. Guess I am not too young to learn something new in this business," Billy stated.

Back at the motel, Captain Nix gleamed through the society page. He noticed that a 'black tie' event was to take place at the Plaza on Friday night. Several directors were being honored for their continued service to the administration. The directors were listed in no particular order, but one jumped from the page. The CIA Director was on the list.

"Look at this Billy. The CIA Director is being honored for his services," showing Billy the article and list of honorees. "It's going to be held downtown at the Plaza. "This will be our best opportunity to take care of business. Tomorrow we will survey the Plaza and the adjacent buildings."

Early the next morning, they drove the few miles to DC. As they approached the Plaza, Nix slowly moved in front of the Plaza, allowing Billy to take pictures out the window. Driving down to the next light, Nix made a U -turn, continuing up the street to a parking lot a few blocks from the Plaza. He stopped at the entrance, picked up a ticket and proceeded to find a parking spot. Both men slid out and walked the few blocks, surveying every crack and cranny to see what best suited their purpose. It was nearly eleven when they finished and aimed the car down the road to the motel. On the way, he stopped at a Panda Inn, picked up some Chinese food to eat back at the motel.

Munching on the food, Billy stated, "I got some really good shots. We'll view them as soon as I finish this bowl of noodles."

Dean opened the camera, scrolled through several scenes, "here's the best ones," he said. Holding the camera at an angle, Nix was able to get a better view. Captain Nix scribbled some notes, drew a diagrams on a note pad. "Our best option will be at the end of the event."

Smiling, "I guess they will be pretty loaded after all the toasting," Billy said.

"Billy, I need to get you inside. Maybe you could be a bus boy or server. You will need to identify the CIA director."Thursday afternoon Captain Nix and Dean drove to an equipment rental company. Nix picked out a large truck with a boom. "This will do the trick. We will pick it up Friday afternoon after three," he told the clerk.

On the way back to the motel, they stopped at an office supply store. Nix picked out two large pieces of board and had the clerk print zzzzBest Telephone Service and a local telephone number.

Their next stop was a thrift store.

Captain Nix picked out a pair of work shoes, a baseball cap, a dark blue jacket and a pair of coveralls. "Guess we are ready for the party," he said.

At three in the afternoon, Captain Nix picked up the truck and drove it to an alley not far from the Plaza. He attached the signs on each side of the doors and proceeded to drive to the side street opposite the entrance to the Plaza. He parked the truck and placed several orange colored cones in front and behind the truck. Stepping down, he walked around the corner and met up with Dean.

"Let's get a quick bite to eat before we take care of business," Nix said. They walked a short distance and came to an alcove which had a sub sandwich shop, a jewelry store and a boutique. They bought the subs, chips and a soda and set at a table under a large bright red umbrella.

Billy couldn't contain himself, laughing.

"What are you laughing about?" asked Nix.

"It's amusing and funny at the same time. I was just wondering what the hell this blank, blank president is thinking about all these killings." Billy chocked on the next bite . . . hurrying to wash it down with the soda.

"One thing for sure. He's mad as hell. No doubt about it," Nix chuckled. "Guess we will just have to give him one more thing to worry about."

Billy shook his head, wiping the smile away.

The sun was setting, causing the evening twilight to cast shadows along the street. Dean walked across the street, standing in front of the entrance to the Plaza. He paused, cleared his throat and walked inside. The DC Plaza, was a 5 star Hotel with all of the amenities . . . brightly lit chandeliers hanging from the ceiling, Italian marble flooring and hand carved wood railing. The soft leather chairs and sofas were spread out for reading or focal points of conversation. One section included; a news/magazine/gift shop, barber shop, ladies salon and at the corner, a large smoking lounge for guest, plus an interesting bar, set in a horseshoe. The wall to wall mirror on the back wall of the bar reflected pictures of Presidents, Congressmen, Congresswomen and dignitaries who were either guest or consulted business in the Hotel.

Walking to the newsstand, Dean purchased a newspaper and two magazines, and then found one of the large leather chairs, facing the hallway that led to the convention room. Hearing chatter and laughter, Dean peered over the newspaper, watching as several guest entered the lobby and file down the hallway. Three men, dressed in business suits, entered. Dean quickly pulled a picture from his jacket. Glancing at the picture, the one in the middle was the CIA Director. He watched them stroll down the hallway, open the door and disappear.

Meanwhile, Captain Nix walked to the truck.

Sitting inside, he changed clothes and opened the black case, exposing the difference pieces of the weapon. Taking it out, he carefully erected each piece, checked the scope and firing pin. He glanced at his watch. "Time to put this mission into operation," he muttered, as he mechanically set the boom to lift in five minutes. Opening the door, he glanced in every direction before climbing in the boom. "Now, I need to wait until Dean gives me the signal the director would soon walk through the door to the waiting car.

Nix placed the weapon to his shoulder, focused the sights and lay it against the wall . . . waiting.

It was after ten o'clock when several men, laughing and jesting, walked down the hall to the lobby. No sign of the director. Standing, Dean placed the newspaper under his arm and strode to a different spot for a better view. The director appeared alone . . .talking on his cell phone. Dean quickly walked out the double doors, lit a cigarette, the signal that the director would soon walk through the door.

Nix placed the weapon to his shoulder, focused the sights and waited. The town car slowly moved to the curb, waiting for the CIA Director to appear. When the Director walked through the door, the driver made his exit and rushed to the other side to open the back door.

Another guest appeared along side the director, laughing as they made their exit.

Nix checked the scope—square in the middle—

squeezed the trigger. Like a streak of lightning, the bullet sailed through the air, hitting the target. Nix watched the director fall back against the other gentleman, hitting the ground with a thud.

Panic broke out.

There were screams and shouts, call 911. Some offered medical aid to stop the bleeding, while others tried CPR. The paramedics arrived, supplied what medical aid they could, before hosting the director on a gurney and sped off toward the hospital.

Working his way down the boom, Nix jumped the last few feet to the ground, picked up the cones, throwing them in the back of the truck. Stepping inside, he released the lever to lower the boom to its safety setting. Waiting for the light to change, he slowly pulled from the curb, made a left turn and vanished out of sight.

Billy Dean, standing among the crowd, watched police and security agents question those nearby. He slowly made his exit from the crowd, walked back inside the Plaza. Picking up a newspaper from a table, Dean walked through the side exit into the night air.

The next morning, Captain Nix cleaned any possible evidence in the truck, returned it to the equipment rental company. The desk clerk asked him, "How did it work for you?" "Just fine, I would recommend your company to others in the City," Nix told him. "Thank you. It was a pleasure doing business with you," the clerk said. "Do you need a ride?"

"No thank you. I have to meet someone at the coffee shop down the street. Thanks for offering."

The newspaper rack near the entrance of the coffee shop . . . shouted at Nix as he walked by.

CIA Director Murdered last Night in front of DC Plaza.

The subheading: The CIA director was recently appointed to this position by the President. There's a massive man-hunt on for the killer or killers.

The White House will hold a press conference this afternoon at two o'clock in the Rose Garden.

"It's getting a little too hot around here. Guess we need to catch the plane and head home," Nix said.

They gathered up all their belongs, leaving nothing behind to incriminate them. They dropped the rental car off and boarded the evening plane.

Chapter 27

The White House
Command Center

The President called an emergency meeting of top directors in his administration. There was the FBI, CIA, HLS, DOJ, DOD and the State Department. The President entered the room, and all the directors stood to their feet.

"At ease, be seated"

Wiping the tears from his eyes, he addressed the group with sadness. "I have received word that my confident, my right hand lady and a real trooper for my agenda, Val Jacobs, was killed in Chicago."

There was a response of "oh no" and then silence from the group. They were still and stiff waiting for the words of the President.

"Ladies and Gentleman, this is an outrageous attack on this administration for my hope and change for America," his voice quivered as his eyebrows rose to another level. "I will not put up with this any longer. We have lost too many good men and women under my command."

"Mr. President, what do you suggest?" asked the FBI director. "What more can we do?"

"Either you are on my side or you are against me.

Which is it?" he demanded "I'm going to put some things in place that has never been done before in any administration.

First, Jack I want you and the FBI to alert every office in the country to be on the lookout for anyone suspicious. I am going to instruct Eric and the DOJ to implement the National Defense Authority Act immediately. We are authorized to detain indefinitely American citizens without charge, trial or access to legal council. You will work closely with NSA and monitor all telephone calls, emails, social networks of any and all citizens that may be working to undermine my agenda. That includes Tea Parties, Rush, Shawn, Michael, ACLJ, Southern Media, Fox and any news reporters that defy my rulings."

There was an eerie demonic gaze in his eyes and his mouth trembled as saliva flowed down his chin. He wiped his mouth and chin. "I want those bastards no matter what the cost."

In the Oval Office the next day, the President signed an executive order calling for each State's National Guard to duty. The President stated, "The purpose of this order is to restore faith in the government, that security and safety is our prime concern."

"The Guard will monitor our largest cities in conjunction with the exercise program of our Army under the direction of the Department of Defense. The Army will be doing maneuvers, going from house to house and business to business. This program will simulate an invasion of foreign or domestic forces and we need to determine how best to fight this guerilla war."

"I will address this issue from the Oval Office to-morrow morning," he said.

"Isn't this unconstitutional?" the Chief of Staff asked the President.

"In a roundabout way, it is. However, Congress has given me the authority under the NDAA to act in the best interest of our citizens. As I said, I will address this issue tomorrow morning."

Chapter 28

From the Oval Office
The President of the United States

"My fellow Americans, by now you are aware that my administration has been under siege by a group of rebels or terrorist. They have killed many of my top administrators.

It is with reluctance that I have called the National Guard into service. Over the next few months you will view the Guard and our Army in field exercises in many of our major cities. Be assured that this is necessary to protect the government and our citizens from those terrorist attacks and secure your safety. They are rebels—Tea Party members, Rednecks, Southern Hicks, Second Amendment rebels, Bible believers and even many of our Veterans—they despise our mission of hope and change. I want to thank you, the citizens of America who voted to give me four more years to clean up the mess my predecessor left me. In fact, my fellow Americans, it will take more than eight years to turn the country around to my liking and I have heard rumors that some senators are submitting bills to allow me to continue my work after the eight year term.

Now, I know this is contrary to the Constitution,

but with a two thirds majority of the states ratifying this, I could serve you more than eight years. Please be patient and give me the time to change America. I saved General Motors. I saved the major banks and Wall Street. I pushed and saved Obamacare. My next goal is to save the earth with climate change and use the EPA to fight every polluting industry in America. I have already pushed the coal industry through the EPA to close those coal producing mines or make it so expensive to upgrade they will give up and stop fighting me. Of course a few jobs will be lost but like my Secretary of State said recently, "What difference does it make."

"God bless you and God bless America.

The President turned around and spoke again to the citizens. *"You may have to give up some of your freedom and liberty in order to secure your safety. I will be addressing the United Nations next week about the use of chemical weapons in Syria and our First and Second Amendment rights under the Constitution. I personally believe the Constitution is a 'living document' that changes with the times."*

He continued. *"The United Nations through the OIC wants to push 'hate speech' and also they are interested in controlling the sale and ownership of certain weapons. I agree with this and instructed my UN Ambassador to pursue this and bring it to my desk for my signature."*

If the Senate will not endorse these policies and the House will not relent and allow me to use the 'capital' I earned being elected for a second term as your president, I will turn to my executive orders and the mighty pen to get the job done . . . right."

He paused, *"And I want you to know and understand that everything I do is for your freedom and safety. May All....huh, I mean God continue to bless America.*

Chapter 29

Ashville, NC
Command Center

Two sedans moved slowly down the tree lined driveway leading to the colonial home, a restored plantation home of one of the founders of Asheville, millionaire William F. McKinley. Each sedan stopped in front of the entrance, letting the occupants departed from the automobiles and quickly walking to the door.

Opening the door, the butler invited the men in, ushering them to the library where McKinley III was waiting.

McKinley stood to his feet. "Welcome," reaching out to shake hands with the four leaders of Southern Media, General Boyd, Colonel A. J. Jackson, Stonewall Jackson and Jim Coke, the black Senator from South Carolina.

General Boyd opened the conversation. "We have fulfilled a part of our agenda. There's still more to be accomplished and I have faith in our sharp shooters and others that are helping to salvage and save America from this administration," he said. "Here's a brief of the missions and their results. After reading this, it is necessary that they be destroyed. Captain Jackson will give his assessment of our future agenda and targets."

Captain Jackson opened his briefcase, shuffling through some papers; he finally pulled out a chart and passed copies around. "First of all, we do have several more targets. If you will turn to page two, there's a list of twelve targets, however four or five will have to wait until sometime in the future.

Senator Coke spoke up, "Why do we have to wait on these four or five?"

Number one on the list is a Supreme Court Justice. She advocates a change in our Constitution. While speaking during an interview on an Egyptian television set on January 30, 2012, she spoke these words and I quote, "I would not look to the U.S. Constitution if I were drafting a constitution in the year 2012. I might look at the Constitution of South Africa, a fundamental instrument of government that embraced basic human rights." She has also leaned toward using international laws in judging some of the cases that come before the Supreme Court. She is one of the most progressive and dangerous persons on the court today."

"I understand all of that, but why not put her out of her misery?" asked the Senator.

"Let's look at like this. If she is eliminated, this administration would place someone a lot younger on the court. They would be on the court for the next thirty to forty years. Yes, we'll have to abide our time and pray she doesn't die or resign while this administration is in power," he said. This current president is no different in his thinking as well. Recently he mentioned that the Constitution was just a piece of paper. He continued by saying that the Constitution was a living and breathing document. There's a progressive movement in the shadows that are determined to update and change it to their standards.

Let me read you a part of this article by a Harvard University Professor. *"For 30 years conservatives have hi-jacked the Constitution and we want it back."*

The movement has a generic name—*democratic constitutionalism.* It came into focus in 2008 and is bank-rolled by the extreme leftist, Georg Staples, who by the way is no longer among the living."

This brought a few smiles and chuckles.

Jackson went on . . . sharing with the officials all that were on the list: cabinet members, congress, union officials, elitist EPA and NWO and others that stand in our way. We will take one at a time. If we cause enough chaos and confusion in the leadership of this administration, they will become a lame duck. That is to our advantage in taking back our country.

Senator Coke spoke up, "I understand, from reliable sources, that the President has already instigated the use of NDAA. That means some of us here are on that list."

"Thank you for that information, Senator. We'll cross that bridge when we come to it." General Boyd said.

Reaching for his briefcase, the General shuffled through several pages, pulling out a single sheet of paper.

"Gentlemen this is a brief history of our founding fathers. Freedom is not cheap. Freedom cost. We enjoy our freedom and liberty because of their sacrifice and many more that fought in previous wars. This message: "What Price Freedom?" was preached several years ago by a close friend of mine."

Foundering Fathers…

American history books fail to tell us of the struggles encountered during the Revolutionary War, a war we fought against our own government, the British Empire.

Fifty six (56) of the men who signed the Declaration of Independence lost everything — five (5) signers were captured by the British, treated as traitors, and tortured before they died.

Two (2) lost their sons, who served in the Revolutionary Army. Twelve (12) had their homes ransacked and burned. Another signer had two (2) sons captured. Nine (9) of the 56 signers fought and died from wounds or hardships.

What kind of men were these patriots?

Twenty four (24) were lawyers and jurists. Eleven (11) were merchants. Nine (9) were farmers and plantation owners. All were men of means and well educated.

Carter Braxton of Virginia: a wealthy planter and trader saw his ships swept from the seas by the British Navy. He sold his home and properties to pay his debts and died in rags.

Thomas McKean: was so hounded by the British that he was forced to move his family constantly. He served in Congress without pay, and his family was kept in hiding. Poverty was his reward.

Ellery, Hall, Clymer, Walton, Gwinnet, Heyward, Rutledge and Middleton: had their properties looted and destroyed by soldiers and other vandals.

Thomas Nelson Jr.: at the battle of Yorktown, his home was being used as the headquarters for the British General Cornwallis and the General quietly urged General Washington to open fire. The home was destroyed and Nelson died bankrupt.

Francis Lewis: his home was destroyed. The enemy jailed his wife and she died within a few months.

John Hart: was driven from the bedside of his dying wife. Their children fled for their lives, while his fields and gristmill were laid to waste. For more than a year, he lived in the forests and caves, returning home to find his wife dead and his children gone.

Morris and Livingston: suffered similar fate.

Is it any wonder that we that belong to the 'over the hill gang,' and perhaps some young adults, get goose bumps when we hear the "Stars and Stripes," and other great patriotic songs?

My pastor friend continued to talk about the great reformers that blazed the trail before us, such as Luther, Edwards, Calvin, and Wesley. In this century, we have men like Billy Graham and Martin Luther King, one ministering to the world and the other, the Civil Rights Movement.

In sharing about the different wars America was involved in, securing our freedom, over nine million lost their lives in World War I, millions more in World War II and counting Korea, Vietnam, Desert Storm and other types of action, thousands more gave their lives.

In closing, the minister spoke on the seven wounds of Christ and what His death cost God, His only begotten Son. What animal sacrifices could not do, the shedding of the blood of Jesus offered forgiveness for all time.

Yes patriots, it will cost—sometimes possessions, family, friends, and lives. Remember the words of that great patriot, Patrick Henry. *"Give me liberty or give me death."*

Chapter 30

Joe Capps &
Shirley Jean

During an altar call at church, Joe went to the front, along with several others to accept Jesus Christ as their Lord and Savior. Ben stood by Joe and breathed a prayer for him.

There was great joy in the church that morning. The pastor stepped off the platform to shake hands with each one standing at the altar, encouraging them to find a place in the family room to his right. Some of our members would like to share with you, give you a Bible, and some important information on your new journey.

"Will you go with me?" Joe asked.

"Of course, this is a wonderful step you've made today," Ben told him, moving slowly toward the family room together.

Sarah Lynn placed her arm around Shirley's shoulder. Moisture of happiness fills their eyes. "I prayed for this day," Shirley said. "I know God's Word talks about not being unequally yoked together with unbelievers."

"I can vouch for that. Ben was raised in church, but when he was a teen, he didn't see the need of it," she told her. "I still married him, but it took years to get him to go to church with me. He loved to hunt and fish. Seems like every Sunday, he would rise early before daylight and off he would go. By the time I got up he was gone. I would get the kids ready and off we would go by our self to Sunday School and Church."

"Whatever changed his mind?" asked Shirley.

"When Sonny was born, he had a heart problem and wasn't expected to live. I believe it was the turning point for Ben. He got real serious with the Lord. I know you are not supposed to bargain with God, but Ben did. He promised to serve him if He allowed Sonny to live and grow up without any health issues," Sarah told her.

"That's an amazing story."

"God is amazing. Guess that is why I love that old Negro spiritual *'Amazing Grace.'* I understand John Newton was in the slave business, when he heard the gospel message. The Gospel made a change in Newton's life, and we rejoice every time we sing it," Sarah told her.

"Can we sing it?" Shirley asked.

While the boys are in the family room, let's go to the piano. I'll play and we both can sing Amazing Grace. Pulling the bench out, Sarah sat down and played a few notes. "Get a song book, behind the first pew, and turn to page 257 . . . Amazing Grace," Sarah told her. She played a few chords and they begin to harmonize. *"Amazing Grace how sweet the sound that saved a wretch like me. I once was lost but now I'm found, was blind but . . ."*

"Now where did they go?" Ben mumbled. Looking around the church, he heard the sound of music. Ben glanced at the piano, seeing Sarah and Shirley singing. Walking slowly toward them, they put their hands together and clapped. Shirley blushed. Sarah laughed.

Holding hands, Joe and Shirley walked out of the church. In the parking lot, Shirley paused. then reached up and kissed Joe on the cheek. "I am so proud of you. So glad you went to the altar and invited the Lord to be a part of your life."

"Thank you Shirley. I feel so much better, like floating on clouds," Joe said.

She smiled, putting her arms around his neck and kissed before entering the truck. "Let's go somewhere and celebrate. It will be my treat," she said.

"There's a small cafe on Main Street. I like it there. It is quaint, quite and well, just the right atmosphere for such a time as this," Joe said.

He drove out of the parking lot, lifted a thumbs up at Ben and Sarah, then drove on Main Street to the cafe. Pulling the truck into the parking lot, Joe slid out and hurriedly walked around to open the door for Shirley. He took her by the hand, "you are special."

Inside the café, the waitress motioned them to have a seat, while she finished talking on the telephone.

They walked to a booth in the back, away from the noise and chatter, sliding in the corner booth.

While waiting for the waitress, Joe reached across

the table, touching her hand. "If it is alright with you, I would like to call on you.

Turning several colors of red, Shirley lowered her head and spoke in a soft tone, so soft it appeared to be a whisper. "Yes, I would like that."

Joe, with a smile and grin asked, "would you like to take a ride to the lake? There are some beautiful spots on a knoll overlooking the water that is breath taking."

"Maybe for an hour or two, I need to get back before dark."

Chapter 31

White House
Conference Room

The President called a meeting with the political leaders of both parties for Friday afternoon. As they entered the conference room, they were seated around the rectangle table by name and rank. The Senate majority leader's seat was next to the president and across from him was the House majority leader's seat. They stand to their feet as the President enters the room.

Be seated. I have several items that need to draw your attention to; I will outline them item by item and at the end we will listen to your approval, objections or any other proposals."

Item 1.

"I have contacted the Attorney General to start an investigation in connection with the Internal Revenue Service on over one hundred ministers who have violated their non-profit status as a church by preaching a political sermon either on the 4th of July or sometime during the election cycle. According to IRS regulations this is a NO-NO. It will not be tolerated. Do I make myself clear?"

Item 2.

"The red line I drew in the sand was really an

International line that had consequences for the world. It was a bluff on my part to get the International community involved. Now don't get me wrong, I will send some type of signal to Syria that we mean business, even though our Secretary of State called it a 'little hit or show of force.' Of course he shouldn't have stated it that way, but I concur with his assessment."

Item 3.

"I have a meeting next week with President Putin. I am sure we can come to some kind of agreement. Putin is a very strong advocate for Syria. A part of the reason for this strong attachment is due to the military base in the gulf. They need the base to export oil and gas to his country. I need your backing as I meet with him."

Item 4.

"There's been a lot of discussion on Fox News about the number of Muslim Brotherhood men and women in my administration. For your information, and I don't want it repeated outside of this room, I don't care what Fox or any other Tea Party group thinks. I am the President."

Item 5.

"We are approaching the budget crisis again. You must raise the debt ceiling and don't even think for a moment that I will not use my executive order privileges to put many of you in your place. I don't care if the debt ceiling is 50 trillion; we have to have the funds to operate my agenda and the change I plan for America."

Item 6.

"I have authorized the EPA do whatever is necessary to implement the rules and regulations that will bring down the "0" zone and climate change about 30% in the next ten years. This will eliminate fossil fuel within five years. All of our energy will come from renewable products, windmills and solar. Of course it will eliminate many jobs, but that is one of the side effects of breathing clean, fresh air. The workers that are affected by these changes can be guaranteed that the government will take care of them with subsidies, welfare, entitlements and of course Obamacare. Mr. Bain, as the majority leader of the House, you must pass my agenda."

Item 7.

"Gentleman I have been fighting an uphill battle with the American public on all of these 'phony' scandals. I need you to stand with me on 'Fast and Furious,' 'Benghazi,' 'IRS,' and the 'NSA.' I am your President and Commander in Chief."

Item 8.

"After my Head of State meeting with President Putin, Michelle and I will be leaving for a forty five day vacation. First to Aspen, Colorado for a winter breeze, then we will fly to Hawaii—my birth place—and then to the Orient. If time permits we will take in the wonderful countries of Europe — France, Italy and Spain.

Item 9.

"I know I am leaving the welfare of our country in

good hands. So fight it out and come up with a budget that I can sign when I return. This is my agenda and I will not be taking any questions or comments at this time. You are dismissed.

The Senate majority leader, under the control of the democrats, turned to the group and said, "I approve of what the President said. Now we must come together and figure out a budget that the President will sign. Mr. Bain it is up to you in the House to muster your troops and come up with a budget that the Senate can agree with."

The entire assemble of whipped leaders, except the Senate speaker, walked out of the meeting with their heads hanging low.

Chapter 32

IRS
Internal Revenue Service

The Internal Revenue Service in Los Angeles, Miami, Chicago, Seattle and Charlotte North Carolina are in full swing, ready to pounce on the churches and ministers that preached political messages to their congregations either on the 4th of July or just before the election of national offices. They obtained DVD's and transcribed messages, which had been forward to the IRS by local pastors.

The LA office has charted a course of action against a pastor in Chino Hills, California. According to their records, this pastor addressed his congregation to vote the Biblical way and he also had some radical speakers from Act for America Network—involved in educating the citizens of the agenda about the Muslim Brotherhood and their political aim of subrogating infidels to either convert to Islam, jizah (a heavy tax and second class citizen rate) or be killed.

A large military vehicle with 8 SWAT team members dressed in battle dress uniforms, helmets and face covering balaclava hoods jumped from the military vehicle with their assault weapons in operational mode.

Four black unmarked cars raced to a sudden stop behind the SWAT vehicle. Sixteen men, dressed in bullet proof vest, slid out of the cars. With weapons drawn, they raced through the church parking lot to the entrance of the chapel.

Approaching one of the ministers, they pushed him to the ground, striking him several times to the face and body and handcuffed him.

Slamming the door of the church office open, several officers rumbled through the receptionist room, pushing the secretary up against the wall. A battery ram knocked the pastor's door from its hinges, allowing the swap team to ransack the office, picking up computers, files and turning over incidental bookcases. They marched out, waving their weapons, carrying what items they could secure under their arms.

The receptionist, scared and crying, finally was able to call the pastor. Sobbing, "They came in like the Gestapo, waving guns and ransacked your office," she told him.

"Did they have a warrant?" he asked her.

"I really don't know. They just busted in through the door, pushed me against a wall and headed for your office."

"Ok Sue, I want you to take the next couple days off. I will stay in contact with you and have you give a report and statement of facts to the authorities," he told her. "I will handle it from here on out. They haven't heard the last of this." As Pastor Johnson walked out of the office, several neighbors ran across the parking lot. One held up his cell phone while another lifted his I-Pad.

Reverend Johnson, we have most of this on video. The SWAT team and the four cars, all with their weapons drawn, heading toward the chapel office.

"Thank you," he said. "That will be a big help when this is spread over the internet, TV, blogs and the newspapers."

Later that day several local stations from Los Angeles along with reporters from the local newspapers invaded the parking lot. They were now in a position to report this outrageous attack on a Christian church. There was much ado about the outrageous search and seizure of computers, files and personal papers.

This is Sam Jones reporting live from the parking lot of New Hope Chapel in Chino Hills, California. My understanding thus far, the IRS in conjunction with the local police and sheriff's department swept down, unannounced, and invaded the church, confiscated computers, files and other material. This is my personal observation, "this is exactly what President Obama promised. When you mess with him and his agenda, watch out. He will take you down or seek the dogs on you." He paused, seeing Pastor Johnson walking toward the reporters.

"Pastor Johnson, Pastor Johnson. May I ask you some questions?" Jones asked.

"First, I want you and your crew to walk though

the office and view the damage these officials did."

The Fox crew, plus other reporters were led through the office, taking pictures and video of the damage. After many of the reporters on the scene, had observed the damage, taking pictures and videos, pastor Johnson was now ready to make a statement. They walked out of the office and stood in the parking lot.

Fox, ABC and Channel 11 turned their cameras on the pastor as he began to speak. "Ladies and gentleman,. this was an outrageous attack on my first amendment rights under the Constitution. There's absolutely nothing in the Constitution that tells me I cannot speak on political matters from the pulpit. When Senator LB Johnson was close to losing the senate race in Texas, he submitted a bill that would make it illegal for non-profits to become involved in the political process. Now there's an IRS code that stipulates a pastor can not endorse a party or person for office. Nowhere does it state that I can't speak about the evil of this day and the corruption in high places."

"Pastor Johnson are you going to file a complaint with the IRS and your local representative?" A reporter asked.

"I will file a complaint with my Representative in Congress by email. I will follow this up with a phone call and a special delivery letter."

"Do you think the IRS will nullify your non-profit status as a church?" another reporter asked.

"If they want a fight on their hands, I have over one hundred pastors in the same boat, and we will give it to them. This is not some Muslim Sharia or Communist country—this is still the United States of America. We still believe in the Constitution and will defend it to our last breath. My church stands for 'freedom and liberty' for for all Americans. And you can quote me on the air and in the newspaper, this is not some communist, socialism or Muslim country— this is still the United States of America."

With that last statement, there was a loud applause from those standing in the back ground.

"Thank you Pastor."

This is Sam Jones reporting live from Chino Hills . Now back to you in the studio.

Chapter 33

Colonel Jackson
Captain Nix
Governor of Texas

Captain Nix picked up the ringing cell phone. "This is Nix." He answered. Captain this is Colonel Jackson. "Captain I need you to fly to Austin, Texas and meet me at the Embassy Hotel on Alamo Boulevard. That's all the information I can share with you at this time."

"Am I to come alone or should I inform Billy Dean?" he asked.

"No. This is a job for you and me to handle. It is more of a diplomatic job."

Captain Nix boarded the airplane in Atlanta, taking the three hour trip to Austin. Making his way through the airport, he walked through the double doors that led to the taxis parked in the yellow zone.

Throwing his bag in the back seat of the taxi, he entered and said, "Embassy Hotel on Alamo Boulevard."

"Yes sir," the driver replied. When the taxi pulled in front of the Embassy canopy, Nix picked up his bag, slid out and paid the driver. Walking through the double doors to the lobby Nix turned his head in all directions, looking for his contact. Not recognizing anyone, he moved swiftly to the reception desk and asked if Colonel

Jackson had checked in.

"Colonel Jackson is in the Alamo Dining Room. He is expecting you. The Alamo is directly behind us. Take a right turn by the Café and you will find the entrance to the restaurant. The hostess will lead you to Colonel Jackson's table."

Captain Nix stood still at the table. A moment elapsed. Colonel Jackson looked up and invited Nix to have a seat. "I have already ordered. When the waiter comes back, please order whatever you like."

"Sir may I ask or inquire what our mission is?" Nix asked.

"This is not the place to discuss business—not the business we are in. I will go over the details later tonight. I will tell you this much, we have an appointment with Governor Nelson tomorrow morning at eleven."

After dinner, both men walked out of the restaurant and took the elevator to the seventh floor. Jackson used the security card and entered the room. It was a large open area with two double beds, a wet bar and a large bay window that exposed the city lights.

Colonel Jackson opened his briefcase and laid out several graphics and pictures. "Tomorrow morning we are presenting a plan to the Governor that outlines our objective in taking back our country. Governor Nelson is a real patriot and recently he won reelection with 67% of the popular vote."

"And just how do we do that? I know we have

made dents in this administration and the President is worried and upset at losing so many of his friends and cabinet members." Captain Nix asked.

"I am going to show you a small sample of our strategy. We have Brigades in nearly every Southern State and a few in the Mid-West. At the present time we have several governors on board. Governor Nelson is our top prospect and goal. If we can bag him, it will be a feather in our cap and many more will come on board."

They rose early the next morning and ate breakfast in the Hotel's City Café. After leaving the Café, they walked through the lobby door. A strong breeze swept through the trees, causing Nix to look up, noticing the sky was filled with black/white clouds.

"This is some sight, huh," Nix said. "If the clouds burst forth with rain, it will remind me a lot of Atlanta and the South. It seems like it rains every afternoon—so much that when the sun comes out there's a vapor rising from the asphalt or concrete roads."

They walked back inside, taking the elevator to the seventh floor and their room. Once inside, both men took turns freshening up. They checked each other's attire, suits, ties and polished shoes.

They entered the lobby and waited for their automobile to be brought to the front of the Hotel. Colonel Jackson passed a fin to the bell hop, slid in under the wheel and began their drive to the Governor's office.

Security was tight at the Governor's office. Both

men had to show identification, go through a security point for weapons, and finally entered the lobby of the Executive office. They smiled at the receptionist. She returned with the smile and a warm Texas greeting, "Welcome to the Texas White House." The Governor is expecting you. Please have a seat and I will let the Governor know you are here.

The double doors, beautiful hickory stained wood with glass etchings of the Alamo and Sam Houston in the center, swung open. A tall beautiful blond, with hair flowing down each side of her face, greeted them.

"Please come with me," she said. She opened the door to the Executive office and invited them to have a seat. "The Governor is on the telephone. He will be with you shortly."

They walked toward a large black leather couch, stopping a few feet from the couch and gazed at the wall. It was covered with pictures of early settlers of Texas—pictures of Sam Houston, Jim Bowie, Davey Crocket and some of his Tennessee Volunteers and the Alamo. They sunk down in the leather cushions. Captain Nix pointed at the large oversized Governor's desk, made of walnut or cherry wood with a glazed finish and marveled at the Texas Longhorn hanging on the wall behind the desk.

The Governor entered, holding out his hand out to greet them. Please have a seat. Jackson and Nix took the two large leather chairs in front of the Governor's desk. Standing to the side of his desk, the Governor told them,

"Gentleman, I received a telephone call from a good friend of mine, General Boyd. He tells me that you have some information that would be of benefit to Texas."

"Thank you Governor Nelson."

The General is correct in stating this would be beneficial to Texas, as well as the rest of the country.

The General wanted me to relate this story first. A story that relates to America and our demise if we do not rise to the task and fight again for our freedom and liberty.

In 1939, as the Spanish Civil War was drawing to a close, General Mola was making his final plans to attack Madrid. Someone asked him which of his four columns would be the first to enter the city. He responded, "The fifth." His answer became world famous.

General Mola's most important column was a band of rebel sympathizers inside the city. They were already busy at work behind Loyalist lines aiding the Generals cause. Since that time, the term fifth column has been used worldwide to describe traitors who assist the enemy from within.

"Governor Nelson, we have the fifth column in high places, abiding our time when we can strike and secure our freedom and liberty from the forces of progressives and communist—and even Muslims, who have launched their agenda through the Muslim Brotherhood.

They too are abiding their time to strike fear into the heart of unbelievers. *They call it stealth jihad.* This president has many of the Brotherhoods top leaders working in his administration. I have a list of their leaders that I can share with you at another time," Jackson said.

"That's a great story line. It tweaks my interest. Now tell me more about your organization. I have a deep respect and appreciation for General Boyd and feel he is on the right track of changing our government for the betterment of all of our citizens?" the Governor said.

"Sir, we try and keep everything under the radar. The NSA is after some of our members, even the General is under suspicion. A leak (from the White House or other sources) indicates that the President is using the NDAA to round up those that expose him and his agenda."

Colonel Jackson opened his briefcase and pulled out several pieces of paper. He laid them on the Governor's desk, watching as the Governor picked up the papers, leafed through them and inquired what they mean.

"Governor, the graphs shows our sites of operation. We have a great number in the South and several new ones in the Mid-West. This letter from the General will give you some information on our plans. To accomplish our goals, we need to enlist the State Militia. The militia is under your control, and for the time being the Feds have no say in how you use your militia."

"Gentleman I need you to have the General call me again. I will need further information from him before I can commit. I indeed am worried about our country. It has crossed my mind to secede from the Union and become a self supporting sovereign State."

"Now if you will excuse me I have other matters to take care of." He stood to his feet, a tall 6' 4" Texan with steel blue eyes, slight gray in the temples, reaching out his hand to shake. Walking to the door, the Governor opened it, letting Jackson and Nix make their exit.

Walking out of the Capitol building, Jackson turning his head, "This was a successful meeting. I know the General will confirm things and the Governor will come on board."

Chapter 34

NSA
National Security Agency

Without Congressional approval, the NSA is still abusing their authority. They have thumbed their nose at Congress, the courts and the investigative committees, continuing to harass and spy on the citizens of America.

They are still collecting data that could be used against any individual or group that opposes this administration. Under the NDAA, citizens could be classified as a terrorist or rebel, which could place them under arrest. American citizens could be retained as long as the administration deems necessary. Of course, this is against the Constitution—but who worries about the Constitution. The NDAA stipulates that your rights are dung—no lawyers, no Miranda rights and no telephone calls.

A recent story on WFRG-TV highlights an ex-Muslim author and spokesperson against the Muslim Brotherhood and the love affair this President has with them. Shawn suggested that he has become a thorn in the flesh and shared the various ways they can harass you. He told of threatening telephone calls to his person and family. One such call was recorded and as soon as I hung up, the phone rang and they played back my conversation word for word.

The following week on WFRG TV, the host interviewed Eric Dempsey. Dempsey had a recent conversation and interview with the Reverend Jeremiah Bloom. Bloom told him that he helped the president to accept Christianity in theory, without compromising his Muslim faith and upbringing. Bloom also discussed the political arena and the essence of Black Liberation Theology.

"It doesn't surprise me. The president's father was a Muslim, he went to a Muslim school and his mentor was a socialist, while his grandparents were communist," Jackson said.

The undersecretary director of the NSA called the White House about a conversation that was of extreme importance to the administration.

He told the White House switchboard, "I need to talk to the Chief of Staff."

"Just a moment please while I connect you," she said.

"Ok John what is this all about?" he asked.

"Our monitoring office picked up one recent call— "We the People"—which advocated for a State-wide conference. This conference needs two thirds of the State to convene, vote and establish an agenda that would certainly be contrary to the President and his programs for America."

Raising his voice, Jason harshly spoke, "If we are

to achieve our goals for America, we must stop this chatter about a State conference. We need to know who the ring leaders are and how to stop them in their tracks."

"I have the sound tract. I will forward it to you. You need to enlighten the security forces and let the President decide how best to handle this. It should be done under the radar," he told Jason.

Jason responded, "I need you to monitor that site and any other radical conversation talk about a State Conference."

Major newspapers, unlikely sources of information, have jumped on the NSA due to the fact that an AP reporter was under surveillance and his phone calls monitored and recorded. The editorial in the New York Beacon mentioned that this administration is abusing its power and authority. It is turning into a dictatorship with the President at the head and there seems to be no checks and balances. If the country continues to tread down this road—it will self destruct.

Chapter 35

Joe and Shirley
Engagement

Five Months Later

Five months after Joe and Shirley started dating; they drove to the lake, to watch the sunset before it disappeared over the horizon. Opening the door for Shirley, she slid out. "Thank you," she said. Joe took her hand, helping her walk the rugged shore line. Finally, they walked up a small knoll, overlooking the lake. The light wind, moved ripples across the surface, while waves smashed against the shore line.

"What a beautiful site—the lake, the sunset with the hues of orange, yellow and a spot of red," Shirley said. She leaned against Joe's shoulder, watching the shadows move slowly across the water. Pulling a velvet blue box from his pocket, Joe stepped in front, knelt down on one knee, "Shirley, will you make me the happiest man on earth by being my wife. I love you and want to spend the rest of my life with you."

Shirley, with her golden locks hanging down to her waist, a smile on her face — turned several colors of crimson. "Yes, yes, yes. I will marry you Joe Capps."

Standing to his feet, Joe placed the ring on her finger and pulled her tight against his chest. With his arms around her, he kissed her on the cheek, ear lobe and the side of her neck. Stepping back a space, kissed her again and again.

With his arm around her waist, they walked the rugged shore line back to the truck. On the way home Shirley asked, "Can we go by the England's. I would like see Sarah. I know she will as happy as I am about our engagement."

"That's alright with me," Joe said. "I would like to ask Ben to be my best man."

With one arm around Shirley's shoulder and the other one on the wheel, they cruised along at a snail pace.

"Joe at this pace, it will take forever to get to the England's. Can't you speed up a little?"

Joe chuckled.

Chapter 36

Alexander, Virginia
Home of CAIR Director
Washington Office

Mohammad Buelj is the director/co-founder of Council on American Islamic Relations. During the Holy Land Foundation trial, five members of their board were convicted of 108 criminal accounts and sent to prison. CAIR was listed as an unindicted co-conspirator. When the current President came into office, he conveyed the message to his Attorney General to drop the charges against CAIR and their officers. They now have access to the White House and several are on the Home Land Security team.

One of the leading aids for the current Secretary of State has complete Muslim Brotherhood ties and family members that belong to that destructive organization.

Colonel Jackson, it is your job to take care of business. You and Captain Nix will make contact with one of our infiltrators in the CAIR office in DC. He will give you the inside information that is needed to help expose CAIR for the terrorist origination it really is.

Colonel Jackson picked up his cell phone, called the one number that would reach his contact. As soon as the conversation was over he stepped on the cell phone and discarded it in a nearby trash can.

Colonel Jackson and Captain Nix arrived at the Atlanta Airport and parked in a site just off the main parking lot, taking a shuttle to the airline boarding area. The two officers boarded the plan but sat in different sections for the two and half hour trip to Dulles Airport.

They disembarked from the plane and headed to the auto rental section where Captain Nix picked out a non descript white Chevy Cobalt. He walked through the car lot, opened the back door of the Cobalt to place his small suitcase. Looking for Colonel Jackson, Nix noticed him standing near the exit. He stopped, letting the Colonel open the door and slid in. "A motel has already been arranged for us. Looking at the papers, he told Nix what streets to drive.

"Here we go again—in the wacky political city in the country," Captain Nix said.

"I remember the words of our late President in the late 70 and 80's make this remark, "It has been said that politics is the second oldest profession in the world. I have learned that it bears a striking resemblance to the first," Jackson said with a grin.

Early the next morning, the sun was barely coming over the horizon, when they left the motel. Driving along the tree lined street, a picture perfect setting that could be printed in any magazine, with manicured lawns, Azaleas bushes and Southern Hydrangeas.

In the background, a stunning two story white clap board home recently remodeled to show the original intent of the owners during the 19th century. This is the home of Mohammad Buelj, a fighter against our court systems, using American Laws for American Courts. He decries this as racist and Islamphobia and demands that the courts abolish these attempts to harass Muslims.

Nix drove slowly through the neighborhood, marveling at the homes sitting back on well manicured lawns, of the upper crust of society. Approaching a major highway, the sign read, twenty two miles to Washington.

Entering the four lane highway, Nix pushed the pedal to the floor, speeding toward the Capitol, where CAIR's office was just a mile or two from 1600 Pennsylvania Avenue. They drove by the massive building which held several corporation offices as well as CAIR headquarters. Colonel Jackson entered a paid parking structure and parked, then they made their exit from the auto and walked toward the CAIR building.

"Nothing unusual about this set up," Nix said.

"They are hidden among many other corporations in that building. We may as well go back to the motel. We can make connection with the contact that works in the CAIR office," Colonel Jackson said.

On their way back to the motel they stopped at a café for dinner. The waitress seated them in a booth near an extra large aquarium, filled with different sea fish, many with yellow and black stripes while others were red and blue. A small shark was resting on the bottom.

The waitress brought a carafe filled with coffee and several different flavors of cream. "Our special today is Swiss steak, mashed potatoes and vegetables," waiting for their reply. Captain Nix, looked at Colonel Jackson, shaking his head, "we'll take two orders of the special."

"Great choice," she said.

Both officers indulged in a great meal, finishing it off with hot peach cobber topped with vanilla ice cream.

After leaving the café, they were on their way back to the motel when Colonel Jackson said, "Boy that cobbler wasn't like what they make back home. The southern cobbler is filled with more Georgia peaches and the flavor . . .

"What can you expect in DC," Captain Nix said.

They slid out of the car and entered their room. Walking pass the bed table, Jackson noticed the red light blinking on the phone. Colonel Jackson picked up the phone and listened to the message, "Call me as soon as you receive this." Immediately he dialed the code number. "A package has been shipped to you. Your contact will give you the package. Use it at the most opportune time."

Nix spoke up. "I guess the fun is about to begin. When and how do we take care of business?"

"We need to talk with our contact at the office. I will try tomorrow morning. We need to be careful so as not to give the mole away."

The next morning, the Colonel made the initial contact with the mole. "I have a package for you. It's in a locker at the Greyhound Bus Station on Capital Avenue. I'll be at the Bus Station at five o'clock, wearing a red plaid shirt and a baseball cap with the Nationals on it. Look for me in the newspaper stand.

The Officers left the motel, driving the short trip to the café. Entering, they smiled at the waitress.

She smiled, "Okay fellows, what do I owe this honor to?" she asked.

"I guess it was your smile, good manners and kind words," Nix responded.

"Have a seat and I will be with you as soon as I turn in this order." She returned with a carafe of coffee and a bowl of different creamers. She smiled, showing her dimples, her emerald green eyes danced like stars, asking, "What would you like?

Both men in a daze . . . looking at this Asian beauty, "What did you say?"

"Would you like to order now or should I come back in a few minutes?" She turned and walked away. Both Officers took another look at her before picking up the menu. Captain Nix picked out a creamer and poured it in the cup, stirring it with a spoon before swallowing a couple sips.

"I am ready to order, how about you Colonel?"

"It says here that you serve breakfast all day. I guess I will order number 4—a cheese omelet with Spanish sauce, red potato home fries and sourdough toast."

"That sounds good to me. Make it two."

When the waitress returned to the table they were ready to order. Nix spoke up. "We'll have two orders of number 4 with sourdough toast."

"Thank you gentleman, I'll turn your order in and bring back some more coffee." She walked away as 'four eyes' watched every move.

After their meal, they left the café and drove downtown. The traffic was bumper to bumper, "just like Atlanta in rush hour traffic," Nix muttered.

They finally reached their destination, pulling in front of the Bus Station. "We only have fifteen minutes to park here," the Colonel said. "I will go in and find our contact while you wait in the car. We do not need a ticket."

He slid out of the auto and walked into the station. He glanced to the left and then the right. He walked through the station, eye balling each person. Standing in the corner of the newsstand, was a man dressed in a red plaid shirt and a baseball cap, reading a magazine. Colonel Jackson entered the small newsstand, picked up a Southern Living magazine and casually walked near the man. He lifted the magazine up in front of his face and spoke a code word. The mole returned the conversation with a code word. Reaching in his pocket, the mole pulled out a key. "I'll pick up the package and give it to you outside." Jackson paid for his magazine and walked through the lobby, taking a seat near the lockers. Opening the locker, the mole pulled out two black cases, placing them under his left arm and continued to walk toward the exit. Standing, Colonel Jackson laid the magazine on the seat and headed for the exit.

"There's more information at a different location. I need you to follow me. My auto is just around the corner," the mole said.

Captain Nix started the car, made a right turn and waited for him to pull out from the curb. On the other side of town the mole parked in front of a Postal Package/Mail Box Service. He made his exit and walked through the door, greeting the clerk. "I have mailbox 1207. I understand I have a package. Here's the slip I found in my box." The clerk searched through several shelves and finally found the package. He had the mole sign for the box, while he waited on another customer. "Thank you," he said, picking up the package and walked out the door to the waiting car.

"This information about CAIR and their operations will knock your socks off," he said. "I have been working undercover for nearly a year. There were some questions on how to dispose of classified material, so I suggested that we shred the documents. Another mole and I went down the back stairs to shred the documents. We were using a small office shredder, which would have taken hours. I marched back up stairs and told the director that it would take forever using the small paper shredder.

"There's a place across down that could destroy all of these documents in a matter of two hours," he said. So we boxed all the loose ones and carried them in a van to the Shedder Store. We stopped by a print shop, went through the dumpster, picking up reams of used paper and had them shredded. With the receipt in hand, we returned to the office, turned in the receipt and no one was the wiser."

"What a great job. We can use this to help bring down this house of cards—CAIR," Colonel Jackson said.

The mole slid out of the back seat of Nix's car and entered his. He drove off and vanished out of sight in the twilight of the evening.

Captain Nix started his car, pulled from the curb and aimed back to the motel. Colonel Jackson leafing through some of the papers remarked, "This is some story," placing them back in the folder. "I'll wait until we get back to the motel to digest more of these secret papers."

"Do you think we should call in, we may not have to continue with our mission," Nix asked. "This material may be all we need to plant the idea and concept that CAIR is a foreign lobby firm that is detrimental to the safety and security of the United States."

In their room at the motel, Jackson picked one of the cell phones from his baggage and dialed the number.

The party on the other end answered with a code name. Colonel Jackson responded in kind. Jackson explained what they had in their hands and waited for a reply. When he hung up, he stepped on the phone and watched it break into a thousand pieces, before tossing it in the trash container just outside his room.

"Guess we can go home," the Colonel said.

"If we play our cards right, we can really blow this thing wide open—and close them down. Just maybe, send these thugs packing or to prison."

After picking up their belongings at the motel they headed for the airport. On the way they stopped at a UPS office to ship a box home, returned the rental car and walked through the airport to their loading zone where they walked through security, without a hitch, and boarded the plane.

"We'll be home in two and one half hours," Nix said. "It looks like this was a successful trip after all.

"I'll make contact with the powers that be and turn all this information over to them to decipher. I am sure we will be hearing a lot about this, not in the mainline media, but other conservative stations will be glad to glance through this," Jackson said.

Chapter 37

Joe and Shirley Jean
wedding

Mr. and Mrs. James and Devonna Williams
cordially invite you
To the wedding of their daughter
Shirley Jean Williams
To
Mr. Joseph Capps
on
Saturday December Tenth
Two Thousand and Thirteen
at Two O'clock in the Afternoon

Faith Assembly of God Church
30th and Cumberland Avenue
Bluefield, Tennessee

After several months building their relationship to a high pitch, Joe finally popped the question. "Shirley Jean will you marry me?" he asked her while kneeling on one knee.

She was so excited by the ring that was about to be placed on her finger, shouted, "Yes, yes, yes. I'll marry you."

The day of the wedding finally arrived.

Shirley Jean wore a awesome full length white wedding dress, with a train several yards long, a bouquet of yellow and white roses and a Cinderella head band with a sheer net covering her beautiful smile. Her blond hair reached the center of her back.

The three bridesmaids wore long pastel yellow evening gowns and carried a bouquet of yellow and white roses. Ben and Sarah's daughter Bonnie was the little flower girl while their son Sonny, the ring bearer.

Joe, dressed in a dark navy blue pin stripe suit, white cuff link shirt accented with a light blue bow tie. His black shoes were spit shined. Ben and the other men in the party were dressed in navy suits, cream colored shirts and bow ties of blue and yellow.

As the wedding march started, the congregation stood to their feet, watching Shirley, on the arm of her father, walk slowly down the center aisle. Reaching the front, Shirley kissed her father, while Joe walked off the platform to take her hand. They continued up the steps, standing before an arch way that had been decorated with green ivy and white roses.

The minister read a short prayer and spoke to both Joe and Shirley, with words of encouragement. "Joe and Shirley, there are what I consider the 4 C's of a successful marriage. The first C is Communication, the second one is Christ, the third one is Commitment and perhaps the hardest one is Change. Throughout your marriage you will experience all of these during your marriage."

He paused . . . Letting the words sink in.

Then the minister shared with them the story of building a fire in a fireplace or a pot belly stove. "In the cold winter months one must bank the embers on the side on the grate and early in the morning place new wood or coal on the embers. There will be cold spells in any marriage. The secret is to not let the fire die out. Always find a way to place new fuel into your relationship."

The rings please.

Sonny lifted the cushion up, letting the minister untie the ribbon and handing the ring to Joe. He spoke to Joe about the circle, the purity of the gold and the promise Joe is making before God.

The minister, turning to Shirley, handed her the ring. Again, he spoke of the importance of the circle, purity of gold and the promise.

After repeating their vows, they sealed it with a kiss. Turning to face the congregation, the minister said, "ladies and gentleman, it is my honor to introduce to you, Mr. and Joe Capps."

At the conclusion of the ceremony, the attendees were invited to meet at the city community center for the reception.

Chapter 38

Secretary of State
John Berry

"This is Colonel Jackson," answering the cell phone.

"This is General Boyd. I am calling about a serious problem that existed over the weekend at the United Nations. Secretary Berry flaunted in the face of Congress and signed the UN resolution calling for a ban on certain weapons. I know he was under the direction of the president, but nevertheless, he is a menace to our cause. I am assigning you and Captain Barnhart to take care of business. Way back in the 60's I made a promise to get this man one way or the other. He was a traitor to the cause of freedom during and after the Vietnam war."

"Sir, are we to fly to DC or should we try and take care of business in Boston?" Jackson asked.

"Do your homework and find the best place and option to take care of this. It matters not if it is in DC or Boston."

Colonel Jackson made contact with Captain Barnhart, suggesting that they meet at the Atlanta Airport on Tuesday morning. "I'll give you more information on the time of our flight and details of our mission."

In the meantime, he made two phone calls to the DC area to set up a meeting with the mole working in the CAIR office in Washington and a motel on the out skirts of town.

Arriving at the Dulles Airport, Colonel Jackson made arrangements for a rental car. Leaving Dulles, he aimed the car to the motel, where reservations had been made. After registering, he picked up the package that had been shipped and entered the room; with dingy dark brown walls, a dark green shag carpet. a small table with a lamp and a double bed . . . strictly out of the 70's.

They smiled at each other.

"Boy it gets worst all the time. At least the last motel had strippers and prostitutes walking the streets," Colonel Jackson said. "We'll contact the mole sometime tomorrow morning after breakfast."

During the early morning hours, the cell phone rang two times. A short pause and it rang again. Colonel Jackson picked up the cell phone.

"Yes."

"This is General Boyd. I am sending two more to the Boston area where Secretary Berry lives. They will contact you as soon as they arrive in Boston. The four of you may need to address this issue together. Jackson hung up the phone, walked to the bathroom and dropped the phone in the basin filled with water.

The local news channel, ABC had a piece on the Secretary of State. The newscaster mentioned the

Secretary would return from his Middle East trip on Thursday. Friday morning he will brief the President and his security team.

"We have a contact in the State Department that could give us the low down on Berry. If he goes home for the weekend we will have a much better chance of taking care of business," Jackson said.

"Let's go have some breakfast," Captain Barnhart said — rubbing his stomach to quite the hungry pains.

While eating breakfast, Colonel Jackson received a call. "This is Davey Jones. General Boyd assigned J.D. and I to your endeavor."

"We are in DC on a mission. Are you our contacts in Boston?" he asked.

"Yes there are two of us. We will survey the area around our victims home—rather compound would be a better description," Davey told him.

"I have a contact in the State Department. As soon as I ascertain the info, I will contact you," Colonel Jackson told him.

They finished breakfast and drove toward the city limits of DC. "I don't like all of this traffic. I hope we can go to Boston and meet up with the other patriots and get this job over with," Colonel Jackson said.

"I've seen Berry out on the water with his sail boat. If he decides to take it out this weekend that would be the best place to take him down," Barnhart said.

Hearing the buzz of his cell phone, Colonel

Jackson pulled the cell phone from his jacket. "Yes."

There was a long pause and the phone went dead. After a short pause the phone rang again. Jackson pushed the accept button and waited for a response. A woman's voice . . . "I am calling to set up our appointment in Boston," she said. "There's a large Metropolitan Mall on Patriot Boulevard, west of town that would be a good meeting place. I will share more when you call."

Colonel Jackson hung up the phone.

"What's wrong now?" Barnhart asked.

Turning red in the face, he stated, "Can you believe they sent a woman to Boston to be a part of our team? Who ever heard of a woman sharp shooter?"

"Did she say where she was from?" Barnhart asked.

"No. She did have a tangy voice — like a Texan or —it wasn't deep southern. Texan I guess."

Barnhart laughed. "I lived in Texas a number of years and some of the ladies were sharp shooters. Better get used to it Colonel. We need all the help we can muster up."

They stopped at a small coffee shop. Sitting in the car, Jackson called a secret number of the patriot in the State Department. When the party answered, Jackson asked, "What news do you have for me.?" he asked.

"I understand after the briefing today, the Secretary will be going home. His wife is throwing a big birthday party for him. This would be your best opportunity to take care of business," the mole stated.

"Great. We will be heading to Boston later today," Colonel Jackson told him. "There's another team already stationed in the area."

They entered the coffee shop. Taking a booth next to a window, they were able to view their car. Sipping on the coffee, Barnhart noticed a man rising from the ground and standing behind their car. "I wonder what he wants or is interested in?" Barnhart stated.

"Keep an eye out while I walk outside," the Colonel said. Jackson left the café, noticing the man bending over, picking up something. He moved quickly through the parking lot and approached the man with a smile. "That's my car. Do you want something?"

"Oh no, I dropped some files and the papers flew all over the place. Some landed near this car. I needed to pick them up—they are legal documents," he said.

"That's okay. May I help you?" Jackson asked.

"I have them all sir. I'll be going. Sorry to have bothered you," he said, rushing to his car.

Colonel Jackson watched the man enter the dark blue sedan. "Hum," Government license plates . . . watching it roar out of the parking lot and vanish in traffic.

"What's that all about?" Barnhart asked, when Colonel Jackson returned to the booth.

"I am not sure. He said he dropped some papers

and they flew near our car. The car he entered was a dark blue sedan, with Government license plates. We need to keep a keen eye on our situation."

After eating, they entered the car and began the journey to Boston. Traveling on the turnpike, Jackson put his finger to his lips and motioned . . . shh. "Why don't you turn some good music on while we enjoy our drive?" Jackson said.

They had driven nearly fifty miles when Colonel Jackson pulled into a rest stop. "Let's make a pit stop and stretch our legs," he said.

While Barnhart was using the restroom, Colonel Jackson walked around the car. Inspecting every nook and cranny, and then looking under the rear bumper, he noticed a small square object. Reaching for the object, it slipped and fell to the ground. He gently picked it up.

"Now what?" he thought to himself.

Scanning the parking lot he noticed a semi-truck, with the driver still inside. He walked through the lot and bent over placing the bug under the wheel well. Whistling a tune, he walked nonchalant around the semi, motioning to the driver with a thumbs up. Pulling 4 quarters from his pocket, he continued walking to the soda machine, inserted the coins and waited for the soda to drop.

Meanwhile, Barnhart, made his exit from the restroom and stopped at the soda machine. He deposited 4 quarters, picked up the soda and both men walked back to their vehicle. Entering the car, Jackson began to laugh, then fear gripped him.

Barnhart noticing the change, "What's wrong now," he asked.

"There was a bug on our car." Jackson said, with a strained voice. "I wonder how they got that information. Do you suppose the NSA has monitored our calls? What about our patriot at the State Department?"

"Give me your cell phone," Barnhart told him. "I must destroy it now." He opened the door, crushed the phones with his foot and walked to a trash can, discarding it. Jackson took a deep breath, letting it out slowly . . . his pulse rate slowly moved downward. He leaned back against the headrest and closed his eyes.

Barnhart continued the drive, slowing down as he neared the Boston city limits. He made a turn into a Rite-Aid parking lot. "Colonel, I need you to get two cell phones from the bag in back." Jackson, shook his head, "what?"

"Get two phones out of the bag on the back seat," Barnhart told him. Jackson slid out of the car, retrieved the phones, and returned to the front seat. Pulling a small piece of paper out of his pocket, he dialed the number on the paper. A woman answered. "This is J.D. On our way in, I noticed a large mall on the west side of town. It is located on Patriot Highway. My partner and I will be at the Subway. It is located on the second floor in the food court. I will be wearing a navy blue pants suit, yellow blouse and a canary yellow flower in my hair."

It was almost closing time for the Mall, when Jackson and Barnhart entered, taking the elevator to the second floor. When the door opened, about twenty feet ahead was a billboard with an arrow pointing to the food court. Walking through several food vendors, McDonalds, China Express, Starbucks, Sharro Pizza, Charlie's PhillySteak, they stopped at the Subway. Glancing at different tables, Barnhart spotted a light brown skinned woman, with long black hair and a canary yellow flower over her left ear. Barnhart moved casually toward the couple, while Colonel Jackson stood to one side. Barnhart was about ten feet from the couple when he smiled, then softly whistling, *"The Yellow of Texas."*

The brown skin lady picked up the tune. Humming a few notes, before rising to her feet and leaving the food court. Colonel Jackson, standing a short distance away, turned his head, watched this beautiful brown skin woman, with a shapely figure and long black hair walk in front of them to the exit.

In the parking lot, she introduced herself and her partner. "This is Davey Jones and I am J. D. McCoy. We are in this together . . . one mission . . . one goal."

Davey Jones spoke up, "we have rooms already booked for tonight. We have done our research. Sometime tomorrow J.D. will find a way to help serve at the party Ms. Berry is throwing for her husband. This will give her the opportunity to survey the situation and give us our clue."

Saturday morning, the sun beamed over the horizon, lighting up the motel room. Colonel Jackson jumped to his feet, stretched his frame and walked to the bathroom. After showering, shaving and brushing his teeth, he walked out and poked Barnhart several times. Barnhart turned over and pulled the pillow over his head.

"Ok buster. Would you like a glass of water on your head?" he asked.

"Okay, okay . . . I'm getting up."

Colonel Jackson opened the door, took a deep breath of the cool air and continued to walk to the front office. Standing in front of the news rack, the headlines jumped from the page; President and Congress at a stand still. The sub headline: *"Who will blink?"* He retrieved quarters from his pocket, inserted them in the slot, lifted the door and pulled out the paper. Walking back to the room, he noticed a beautiful lady standing outside her door. Freezing in his tracts, the gaze was one of awe . . . J. D. was one beautiful Hispanic lady. Mumbling, "What caused her to join and be a part of the Ring of Fire?"

Opening the door, Barnhart walked through the parking lot, catching up with Jackson. "Are the other troopers up yet?" he asked.

"Take a glance to my right. What do you see?" he asked.

"Wow."

"Wow is right." with a grin on his face. "Let's walk over and see if they want to go for breakfast."

J.D. walked back inside and closed the door. Inside her room she opened the sketch of the compound, taking notes of each section: the mansion, the guest house, the garden, the pier and the water.

A knock at the door surprised her. Covering the sketch with some papers, she strode to the door. Pulling the security chain out of its space, she cracked the door. "Good morning gentleman."

"Are you ready for breakfast?" Barnhart asked.

"Knock on the next door—119 and see what is holding up Davey," she told them. "Give me five."

Colonel Jackson walked a few steps and knocked on the door. Davey Jones opened the door . . . seeing Jackson, he excused himself. "I'll be ready in ten minutes."

"J.D. said she would be ready in five . . . get a move on. We are headed for breakfast."

They loaded in one car. On the main drag, it was bumper to bumper. "I didn't realize it would be this bad getting around Boston," Colonel Jackson said. "I read somewhere it is better to park somewhere out of the city and take a bus or taxi downtown."

Captain Barnhart pointed out a small café in the next block. They pulled to the curb, walked down the street to the Bean Pot. "I sure hope they serve a good breakfast. That name doesn't do much for me," Jones said.

J.D. smiled. "Do you think they serve tacos, burritos and refries?"

"Come on J.D., you know you would like some summer sausage, eggs and red potatoes." Jackson said. They all laughed, as they entered the Bean Pot. The young waitress smiled and pointed toward a large booth in the corner. She followed behind with a small menu and gave each one in the party one. She mentioned the daily special and asked what they would like to drink. She returned with a pot of coffee, four cups and a variety of creamers.

"I'll be back and take your orders," she said.

Davey smiled and spoke up, "She's quite a looker and so young. Did you notice her Boston accent? I guess my Texas twang wouldn't fool anyone."

After breakfast they left the Bean Pot and drove to Boston Bay, a short hop from Moon Bay, the home of Secretary Berry.

J.D. "I need you and Davey take a taxi and head up to Moon Bay. Survey the area and find out what is happening at the Berry compound. In the meantime, we will stay close by and see if we can rent a sail boat for a couple days."

Davey hailed a taxi that was stationed in a taxi zone next to the pier. Once inside the taxi, Jones told the driver to take them to Moon Bay.

"Where in Moon Bay?" he asked.

"We are sightseeing, so just drive us around the area. I understand the Berry's live in Moon Bay. Does anyone ever get to see them out in the garden or their entertainment center?" J. D. asked.

"Nay." he answered, while looking through the mirror at his guest. "They pretty much stay to themselves unless they have a huge party . . . you know, a party for some of the big wigs from the area and DC."

"I understand they are celebrating the Secretary's birthday with a big bash," Davey said.

"Yes indeed. The papers were full of this celebration and all the dignitaries that will be in town," the driver said.

J.D. spoke up. "Do you know who's the cater?"

"You gotta be kidding me. With all that pickle fortune, she employs her own chef and staff. I do understand that the Blossom and Party Time are supplying some of the decorations," he said.

"Is there anything else? We would like to take some pictures. so we can show our poor relatives back home how the 'rich and famous' live," J.D. said

"I shouldn't say this. So you didn't hear it from me—understand. They usually contact a personal escort service which supplies the party with some beautiful young girls."

Looking through the rear view mirror he remarked, "Ms. you sure would fit in with that group. They don't have a dark skinned beauty like you," he smiled.

They laughed.

"Do you know the name of the agency? I just might want to apply for a job?" She smiled so that the driver could see her in the mirror.

"I can arrange that," smiling at J.D.

Colonel Jackson and Captain Barnhart secured a outboard boat and a Jet Ski for the weekend. "You are younger than me, so I'll let you have the Jet Ski," the Colonel told Barnhart.

"Thanks a lot. While you are sailing, I'll be in the water most of the time," he laughed.

"This is first time I have been on water in years," the Colonel said. "I wonder how J.D. and Davey made out?"

J.D. stood at the entrance of the Glamorous Beauty Agency. She opened the double glass doors, etched with a picture of a model, and walked to the receptionist desk. A tall redhead, dressed in a tight fitting slink pants suit, showing all of her amenities, walked from another room. "What can I do for you?" she asked.

J.D., dressed in an off the shoulder bright red blouse with deep cleavage, and 70's white hot pants asked for an application.

The redhead took one look at J.D.

"We don't have applications," she said. "Wait a few minutes and I'll have someone interview you."

A woman and man walked from the other room and invited J.D. to follow them. They entered a cozy room with a large red velvet couch, two large matching chairs and mirrors surrounded the walls that exposed a person from all angles.

The man introduced himself.

"My name is Georgie and this is my partner, Victoria. We own this establishment."

"So you are new in town. Where did you come from and how long will you be in town?" he asked while staring at her cleavage.

"I am from El Paso, Texas. I spent most of my time at the "Emerald Club"—a high society escort service across the border. My take was about $5,000 a night. The Club owner took 40% and I kept the balance.

Victoria spoke up. "Well that may work in Texas but we have a different Clientele in Boston. Most of our Clientele are businessmen or political leaders coming down for a good time. At our parties there's no hanky-panky or sexual escapades."

Georgie busted in the conversation, "what you do after the party is over is up to you. We just want to show them a good time and with your amenities it shouldn't be hard."

"We operate on a 60/40 split. You can start tomorrow for the Berry party if you agree. We've never had a brown skinned beauty like you before. This should be interesting," Victoria said.

Saturday afternoon, a limousine picked up ten of the girls from the agency. J.D. was dressed in a form fitted red mini dress, that showed all of her curves, her long slender legs were covered with thigh high white boots. Her black hair was curled, flowing on the left side of her face and the balance on the right was flipped down past her shoulder. Her brown eyes sparkled like shining stars at night.

The limousine stopped at the security gate of the Berry compound. The guard smiled and waved them on. Driving the long curvy driveway, accented with small trees and flowers, the driver stopped at the front entrance of the colonial home.

The girls made their departure and walked to the front door. Entering the home, they smiled while walking through the double French doors, which led to the terrace and garden below. At the foot of the spiral stairway, two large white square columns with lion's head on top, formed the opening to the impeccable garden: 3 large oak trees, their branches 25 feet wide each, formed a canopy for the built-in fireplace, grill and refrigerator. Several guests were dancing on the magnificent Italian tile dance floor to the tunes of a Jazz combo band.

In awe of the splendid of what money could buy, J.D. stood staring at the 30 x 50 white tent, decorated with balloons, kite flyers and a collage of Berry.

Recognizing two of the congressman, she waltzed toward them. One reached his hand out — as if to say— "Come here." The congressman took her by the hand, stepped back a space, gawking . . . ""where have you been all my life?" he asked. "I haven't seen you here before."

J.D. shrugged her shoulders. "I'm new in town."

"Well, honey you've come to the right place for action. All of the wheeler dealers are here to celebrate our Secretary of State's birthday."

"Excuse me a minute. I need to talk with the Congressman from New York. Don't run off."

J.D. stood still for a moment. Spying the refreshment bar, she made her way to the bar and ordered a Virgin Mary. Sipping on the drink, she wandered through the crowd of well wishers, smiling . . . making small talk until the man of the hour made his appearance. A tall gentleman, dressed in a black suit, light blue tie and cowboy boots touched her arm. "Has anyone ever told you how beautiful your eyes are?"

"Of course," she replied.

My name is Joe. "I'm a Senator from Texas. What's your name and where do you come from?" he asked.

"My mom and dad call me J.D." she answered. "I'm from New Mexico."

"That's an odd name. What does it stand for?"

"Just J.D.," she laughed.

"Did your folks run out of names or what?"

She smiled and turned her head.

"They told me to mingle, smile and have fun, so I'll see you around," she said, walking away.

Secretary Berry and his lovely wife, Terry, finally walked through the French doors. Standing at the top of the stairs leading to the garden, they slowly made their way down the stairs to a hand clap and many "happy birthday" wishes.

Berry acknowledged the crowd, with a sign of victory, as he and his wife walked through the garden. He shook many of their hands and laughed as the atmosphere was one of gala, laughter and drinking. A few of the old men tried to pet, kiss and fondle the beautiful escort girls—including J.D.

She flinched.

It was after midnight when some of the party guest began to leave, leaving some of the stragglers nipping at the refreshment bar.

J.D. caught the eye of the chief security gentleman. Flirting with her eyes and a wiggle, she strode toward him. "Hello. My name is J.D. I'm new in Boston. Can you give me some directions on sightseeing? I love the water and would love to have a harbor cruise?"

He was blindsided and stuttered. "I'm, I'm not sure myself," he said.

She changed the subject real fast, like a race car driver changing gears, she turned the conservation about the Secretary's routine on Sunday.

Stricken by her beauty, he mentioned that most Sundays he would take his sailboat out in the harbor for a few hours. That was his way of cooling down from all the pressure and stress.

J.D. smiled. "Thank you. This has been a pleasant evening. I must hurry and catch up with the other girls.

Have a good evening," she said.

On the way back to the agency, J. D. mentioned that her boy friend would be picking her up. Opening her purse, she pulled out the cell phone and made the call. "Honey I should be back at the office about midnight. Now don't be late."

The girl sitting next to her asked, "You just got into town and already you have a boy friend."

"Not really. I came to town to find work. He flew in a few days ago. He is looking for work as well. The economy is so bad for him where we came from, he just had to do something."

The limousine pulled up in front of the agency building. The girls, giggling and laughing about their experience at the Berry's, made their exit — lingering on the sidewalk as J. D. walked across the street and slid inside the front seat . . . reaching over and kissed Davey.

"What's that all about?" he asked.

"Just playing the part," she chuckled.

"Well, for what it's worth, I like it."

Early Sunday morning, the gang of four rose early. Jackson and Barnhart drove to the pier to pick up the rental while J.D. and Jones hailed a taxi and bolted back to Moon Bay. They arrived in town about eight. The taxi driver asked "where else should I take you?"

There's a beautiful spot on a cliff overlooking the Bay. "Can you take us there?" J. D. asked. The taxi driver consented, making his way through several side streets to reach the cliffs, exposing the beautiful bay . . . sail boats and other water craft were moving smoothly through the water.

They made their exit . . .

"The clock is running, if you want me to stay while you enjoy the scenery," the driver said.

Davey pulled out several bills from his pocket, and paid the taxi driver. "Thank you. I think we will stay for awhile and enjoy the view . . . "by the way, what do you think of the view?" Davey asked.

"If I've seen it once, I've seen it a thousand times. No way can I have what these rich folks have. The misses and I have a little bungalow off the main drag in town," he said, with pride.

The morning sun flicked its rays through the fluffy clouds floating overhead, while Davey and J. D. watched intently for Berry to appear.

"There he is?" exclaimed J. D.

The Secretary, briskly walked on the private pier to the sail boat, a 27 foot, Nordia Van Dam Day Sailer. He untied the boat and jumped on board. Raising the sails, he started the motor, backed slowly from the pier and moved into deeper water.

J. D. pulled the cell phone from her pocket and made the call to Colonel Jackson. "The fish is in the water."

"Thanks J. D. If anything new develops, keep us posted." Colonel Jackson climbed aboard the rental boat, while Barnhart was busy with the Jet Ski. They both moved through the choppy water—white foam from the waves moved further apart. The trip up the coast would take thirty to forty five minutes before they reached the scene.

"I sure would like to have a cup of coffee," Davey said. "We should of thought of that ahead of time."

"Sit back and keep your eyes on the Secretary," J. D. told him. She lay back against a large boulder, closed her eyes for a moment. "Davey, did you read about the half million dollar scheme the Secretary was involved in. I Googled his name . . . Berry and his wife, Terry, purchased a 7 million dollar yacht, named "Isabel," and docked it a neighboring state, Rhode Island. Berry saved one half million dollars, including sales tax and a $70,000. annual excise tax, by not docking the yacht in the Boston Harbor."

"Looks like the rich know how to play the game, do as I say and not do as I do," Davey injected. Looking through the binoculars, he spied Jackson and Barnhart speeding to the scene. They moved swiftly around other crafts until they spotted the fish. Jackson pushed the throttle in, slowing the boat, which rocked fiercely through the choppy water. The Jet Ski, with Barnhart saddled on it, came near, picking up the weapon from Jackson.

Speeding through the chopping water, Barnhart

made several figure eights and then moved alongside the Secretary's sailboat, waiting for . . . the Secretary made a sharp right, facing the coast. Barnhart lifted the weapon and fired.

The Secretary fell forward, then backward into the water.

Chapter 39

White House
Security Room

The entire security force entered the room. Waiting for the president, they looked at one another. There was anger and rage on each face.

One spoke up, "The Times said that Secretary Berry was assassinated over the weekend. What in the world is going on? Who will be next?"

The President entered. He raised his arms in disgust. "I received a call Sunday morning that Secretary Berry was killed while sailing near his home."

He pounded on the table.

"This is it. No more pussy footing around. If they want blood I will give it to them. Erik I want your team out in full force. I want you to turn up the heat on the tea party, the veterans, the conservative radio jocks and all other sources that the NSA has under surveillance."

"Yes sir Mr. President," he said.

"Chuck, as the DOD director, I mentioned before about using the NDAA. It is now time to put it in force. I want some heads to roll. Understand."

"Yes sir, Mr. President," he said.

"I want General Boyd picked up. There's several

ministers on my list also. I will give you my 'hit list' later today. Come by the oval office."

"If this doesn't work, then I will call and enforce marital law throughout the land. I have the police power and the mechanism in place to break the back of any resistance to federal authority, legitimate or not. My (PSA) Police State America, is designed to subjugate the populace and root out any remaining resistance. I have placed a 'litmus' test before my security officers, the Joint Chief of Staff and my field officers in the Air Force, Army, Marines and Navy. This test determines who's on my side and who's not."

The test: *"Are you willing under my command orders to shoot and kill American citizens."*

"Sir does this mean you will implement marital law in its fullest form?" one Staff Officer asked.

"I think I made myself clear. If things get completely out of hand, I will take control of America—with this law in effect I will be able to eliminate all opposition to my administration. I will take charge of the media and make it a state run media and it will be possible for me to remain in power way past 2016 and perhaps indefinitely."

This year alone I have fired Generals and some have retired. These are great men who gave their life and time for our liberty and freedom, but they would not compromise their belief in the Constitution and would not adhere to my 'litmus' test. In addition I have fired over 150 high ranking officers and left them hanging, even after serving some fifteen years of more.

"This is My Military."

"But Mr. President the people won't stand for this?" the DOD director said.

"Chuck, I will invoke stage two of our marital law plan. There will be restrictions on travel, free speech and the right to assemble to air grievances against the government. I will take over the internet—eliminating ideas and forming large demonstrations and we will implement a National ID. The ID will include a code that tells our Security Team who is a friend or foe."

"Mr. President isn't this in violation of the Constitution?" the leader of the Joint Chief of Staff asked.

"Admiral, with a rage in his voice, and an evil stare that could pierce the soul of a man, asked "Would you like to leave the room? I fired Generals for less than your question of my authority. Under martial law there is no need for the Constitution. I will set these things in motion and it is up to you and all those under my command to carry out such orders."

"Understood?" he shouted.

"Any one else want to question my authority?"

I told the America people I would transform America and they won't even know what hit them, until it is too late. Those that oppose me will be removed from society, detained and perhaps executed. Those on that list, as I mentioned before, includes preachers, outspoken talk show hosts and anyone on the internet who has opposed or called for my impeachment or trial as a traitor to this great Country."

"Do you remember the words of my trusted friend, Valerie Jacobs after we won my second term?"

"It's payback time."

"Man I loved that woman. She was a dear friend and one that I could count on completely," tears formed in his eyes. He brushed them aside with his hands.

"Now gentleman 'let's rock and roll," the President told them with a smirk and grin on his face.

"Payback is hell."

Chapter 40

Homeland Security
Police force and violation of our
10th Amendment

The spokesperson at a recent Homeland Security proclaimed "that the DHS is no longer concerned with foreign inspired terrorism. They are only going to focus on domestic terrorism, ostensibly against the American people. We have over the last few months purchased over 2.2 billion rounds of ammo and the acquisition of 2700 army personnel carriers. Even local police departments have been able to purchase these high tech toys—which we could federalize them to do the same work of federal authorities—arresting, detaining and killing American citizens. I have it under good authority that the IRS— Internal Revenue Service as well as many other federal entities have acquired several million rounds of ammo."

A question was asked by one of the attendees.

"Do you think they would actually shoot our citizens?"

"Under the command of the President they will follow orders or our weapons will be turned on them."

"No mercy," the President said.

The government could create a 'false flag' terrorist attach which could implement a partial part of martial law like what the police and security teams did after the Boston Marathon. They entered many homes under pretense of securing the scene and if there were others that may have been involved in the bombing. This was against our Constitution, yet a test of wills. Are we willing to trade our liberties for safety and security?

Many large city police departments have been given or purchased for peanuts large Hummers, tanks and other ground equipment to use at their disposal.

Recently the Los Angeles County Sheriff's Department deployed a huge armored vehicle (road warrior) with the sign "Code Enforcement" on the vehicle when they invaded a man's personal home to intimidate him to surrender his property.

American citizens branded as terrorist could be your neighbor, your pastor or even a family member that spouts off about this administration.

HLS has designated Christians, Veterans, Tea Party Members, Gun Lovers, Rednecks, Bible Believers, and Authors that expose this administration and Islam's agenda as potential terrorist.

Chapter 41

July 4, 2015
Washington DC

General Boyd along with several others on the hit list have been detained by the authorities at an undisclosed location.

No charges, no rights, no attorney, no trial.

When the Ring of Fire elite received word of this outrageous act by the President, the internet was on fire with post after post.

Colonel Jackson blew his cover as he called for a million bike ride as well as truckers to invade Washington and cause all the confusion and chaos possible. On his site, he called for "a take back our country battle cry."

The sun was setting on DC when thousands upon thousands of bikers waited a few miles outside the city. The noise of diesels roared, as billows of smoke filled the air, and the semi's lurched forward filling up the interstate and highways leading to the Capitol.

The President called for full military support. "We are under siege and we need your support now," the President commanded.

The DOD director ordered the Navy Seals at the Navy shipyard to proceed to the White House.

The few Congress people still stranded in the Capitol began to weep. Some asked questions while others were searching for ways to escape the wrath that was coming.

Questions floated through the air, like dandelions that have matured, blown by the wind.

"Why did we listen to this President? Why didn't we do more to honor and respect the Constitution? Why did we give in to political correctness? Why didn't we vet this President?"

"Why. Why. Why?"

The Commander at Fort Dix was placed under house arrest. The soldiers would not respond to the call of the maniac in the White House. They had sworn to uphold the Constitution and taken the oath to protect the citizens and shores of America against all foreign and domestic enemies.

When Chuck, the DOD director, caught wind of this insubordination he was angry and threw a hissy fit.

"I'll have their hide," he shouted out loud.

He picked up the secured phone in his office and called the Navy Ship Yard. "I need to speak to Commander Owens?" he said.

"May I tell him who is calling?" she asked.

"Tell him to get his lousy no good for nothing butt on the phone. I want to know where are the Navy Seals."

A long pause—"What's keeping him?" he thought, his mind was racing.

"This is Vice Commander . . . sorry, sorry I can't hear you. We must have a bad connection," hanging up.

The DOD rushed to the White House and entered the Oval Office. Sitting at his desk, the President's head was bowed—as if saying a prayer.

"Mr. President—-Mr. President"

He looked up for a moment and bowed his head in his hands. "I know. I know. The Seals and Army are not coming. Sit down Chuck."

"I, I, his voice quivering, I, I really thought I could offer hope and change to the citizens of America. I wanted so much to change this country in the likeness of Kenya. My father fought the English for years until finally the people were rid of the colonial clutches and chains that kept our people bound for years. So I thought I could make the Constitutional changes that would benefit the people—you know; like hate speech and carrying weapons and there are so many others that are just old stuff."

Chuck broke in.

"Sir, the people love you. You have given so many entitlements and even the Affordable Care Act is a benefit."

"I know. I did my best. Guess it wasn't enough. Why do all those Bush people hate me?" he asked.

"Excuse me Mr. President. Could it be, we have blamed Bush for everything that has happened during the last six years?"

They both laughed.

"Mr. President do you think we could blame this uprising on Bush?"

"I wish we could, Chuck."

"We need to get you to a secure place. All hell is breaking loose in the city. There are thousands of bikers and semi's filling up the interstate and highways leading into the city. There's no way to exit. Do we need to call for the Presidential helicopter?" the DOD asked.

"I want to be sure my family is safe. It matters not what they do to me. Call the secret service and have them take the wife and children to safety. They know where the safe harbor is located," he said.

Chapter 42

Hundreds Die
in DC violence

Washington DC

Backers of ousted President Obama clash with security forces around the nation.

Clashes erupted on Friday across much of the nation between revolutionary forces and supporters of the ousted President, leaving hundreds killed, as rival crowds of supporters of the revolutionary forces and backers of the Marxist President of the United States to mark the July 4th holiday.

The Capitol saw multiple scenes of mayhem as street battles raged for hours in some neighborhoods and in front or near the White House. By evening time, several parts of the city resembled combat zones, with fires burning, black smoke rising and the crack of gunfire piercing the air, thick with tear gas. Streets were strewn with debris and many businesses were ransacked.

Several reporters were able to get information out on the internet — showing bodies lying in the street and scenes showing the floor of an emergency clinic set up to aid those that were injured in the deadliest part of the

the city. Most of the bodies had gunshot wounds to the head or chest.

Other reports are coming in from other parts of the country—Atlanta, New York, Chicago, Miami, Los Angeles and San Francisco. Patriots clashed with local police, buildings are on fire and the freeways and interstates are closed to these cities.

The scene of the fighting contrasted sharply with the carnival atmosphere of the million bikers who invaded Washington Mall during 9-11 in protest of the Muslim march on DC.

The Governor of California has called for the National Guard; however, the General of the Guard disobeyed the order and had his troops stand down.

In an interview with a local Los Angeles news reporter General Hastings stated: "My troops will obey the Constitution and will not turn or use their weapons on the citizens of this great State. I will give up my commission before I buckle down and forfeit the rights of our citizens under the Constitution."

News Flash:

The President of the United States was taken captive earlier today and carried from the White House in chains. The big question, who is in charge of the country. The Vice President can't be found and the next in line has—for all we know and hear—has fled the country. We will update this news flash as more news comes in.

Stay tuned!

NEWS FLASH!

In an interview with Colonel A. J. Jackson, he stated that the DOD director was apprehended along with the President and both men have been taken to a secured location by the Brigade.

"We are searching for the whereabouts of General Boyd, our commander and demand his release along with all the prisoners taken under this President's command. This is still the United States of America and the corrupt leaders in this administration will have their day in court. We still believe in and honor the Constitution."

Chapter 43

America in Shambles

From the Capitol in Washington and throughout the country, America is in shambles. Destruction, fires, looting and gun shots are still being heard in many of our major cities.

The President of the United States has been carried to an undisclosed location. Many of the secret service, loyal to the President, have launched a manhunt for him. There have been off and on gun battles between the revolutionary militia and the secret service.

A small coalition of Senators met at the estate of Major General Ryan Taylor in Virginia. Their discussion centered around the condition of the country, who was at fault and if—only if the country could be saved and what, if any charges could be brought against the President.

Senator Long finally broke the ice.

"We have been fighting a losing battle with this President. We haven't been man enough to stand against him and we have allowed him to use executive orders to damage every facet of our country. Is there enough evidence to convict him of treason?"

"Gentleman, we have 'Fast & Furious', IRS and NSA scandal and we shall never forget the Benghazi killing of four Americans. If those aren't bad enough, we have the president inciting the military and law enforcement officers with the "litmus" test, to fire and kill American civilians. Yes. There's enough evidence to convict him of treason," Senator Long said.

General Taylor, cleared his throat, and urged the men to weigh the facts. "We must try the President in a military court of law. This way we will have the law and military procedures on our side. Impeachment is out of the question. Do I hear a consensus of agreement . . . treason for this President?" he asked.

Each man pondered the question. Finally they all came to the same decision. *Treason.*

General Taylor asked the group another question. "What about some of his staff, and even the leaders in the Senate, can we include them in usurping their authority to create chaos and help cause this damage to our first, second and fourth amendment rights under the Constitution."

"Let's take one step at a time," General Taylor suggested. "We can still reach the present Speaker of the Senate and most of those that promoted the President's agenda. Do we have a consensus . . . take care of the president first?"

Chapter 44

Muslim Uprising
One month later

The Muslim Congressman from Minnesota stood on the Capitol steps and addressed a small coalition of Brotherhood operatives, including the director of CAIR, INA and other agencies under the Muslim Brotherhood umbrella.

"Brethren, today is our day. Today is our time. Today we take over America and fly the Crescent flag over the White House," he yelled.

A shout came from the coalition—"praise be unto Allah."

"While Americans are fighting one another and the country is in shambles, the time is ripe for our people to rise up and claim this country, America, as a Sharia country."

A shout came from the coalition—"praise be unto Allah."

"In 1978-79 the Shah of Iran and his government were overrun and defeated by 'freedom fighters' and established Sharia. I will, in the next few days, invite the President and spiritual leaders of Iran to come and help us select a new spiritual leader in Americastain."

A shout of praise—"praise be unto Allah."

"We have sleeper cells all over the country. In addition there are over 35 homegrown terrorist camps that are ready to slaughter the infidels. Those that will not convert to Islam or pay the jizya tax, will be killed."

A shout of praise—"praise be unto Allah."

"America has been the strong holdout against Islam and world domination," he shouted.

"No more. No more. No more"

A shout of praise—"praise be unto Allah."

Now we will take Canada, India and China—we will establish a caliph just as Allah promised," the Congressman said.

Is this the end of America?

What does the future hold for our families, our children, our grandchildren?

Is there another revolution in the making?

Will the saga continue?

Chapter 45

America, America

General Boyd and all the prisoners taken into custody during the reign of the Obama administration were located and released.

When the General and many of the Bridge, Senators and other leaders that failed to heed Obama's rules and regulations, met again at the estate of General Ryan Taylor in Virginia. They were upset and distraught at the turn of events, then hearing about the remarks of the Congressman from Minnesota.

"We need a strategy set in motion to take back our country. I for one will not surrender our sovereign power to a bunch of idiots that follow blindly the prophet," the General said.

They have vowed through many speakers and their Brotherhood connections to use 'stealth jihad', converting—not with weapons and dirty bombs—but with ideas, court attacks and using our legal and religious system under the first amendment to their benefits.

General Taylor pulled a notebook off the bookcase. "Let me read you some quotes from the leading scholars of Islam and Sharia here in America. Mind you our President and leaders have paid no attention to these ramblings as they still think of Islam as a "religion of peace."

He opened the notebook and began to read quotes of different Muslim leaders.

"The Muslim Brotherhood must understand that using 'stealth jihad', a quiet way of using America's legal and Constitution against her, will help us in eliminating the Western civilization from within and that Allah's religion is made victorious over all other religions."

"We reject the America and all their laws and order. The only relationship you should have with America is to topple it. Eventually there will be a Muslim in the White House dictating the laws of Sharia."

"Let us damn America, let us damn Israel, let us damn the whole world until death. Islam isn't in America to be equal to any other faith but should be dominate. The Qur'an should be the highest authority in America and Islam the only accepted religion on earth."

Aftermath

Revelation,
the end of the Story!
and other Highlights
and Actions in Post
America

Aftermath

Questions that Need an Answer

1. Political correctness on different fronts causes extreme killings.
2. Waivers ban on sending weapons to terrorist under the guise of National Security.
3. Mental illness, not guns the cause of multiple killings.
4. Benghazi
5. Fast and Furious
6. IRS Scandal
7. NSA Scandal
8. President's relationship with Muslim Brotherhood.
9. Why has Obama spent millions of dollars keeping his birth, passport and college admittance and transcripts secret.
10. Will America surrender to 'political correctness' and allow Sharia in our court systems.
11. Will America surrender and become another Islam country in the future.
12. America is at the Crossroads — Will She Survive?

Post America
Revelation, the end
of the story!

The Bible in the Book of Revelation gives us insight and the end of the story from God's viewpoint.

From the studies of the scriptures, and other sources, it is difficult to find America listed in the last days or in the final battle between 'good and evil.' Perhaps one small verse in Ezekiel chapter 38 — possible to contain a reference to America, *"as the young lions thereof."*

Are we destined to become a third world country?

Throughout six thousands years of history, there have been cycles in civilizations, which forced on the people monarchs and dictators. With this in mind, the founding fathers did not want a king, monarch or a dictator to rule over them.

America, as a Republic, is a different breed.

Under the wisdom of our founding fathers they created a Constitution that committed itself to the rule of reason with the power in the hands of the people a Republic with the decree that all men are created equal.

Throughout the world and even now here in our beloved America we find the wind blowing—a perfect storm brewing with progressives, elitist, men of great wealth and men with political power clamoring for leadership or a One World Government. It is not unusual for these types to *sell their soul* to the devil and be possessed with the forces of evil to continue to keep their power and control.

There are several groups — Council Foreign Relations, Illuminati, Bilderberg Group, Tri-Lateral Commission, the Circle and others, all with the mentality of a perfect world controlled by one man as the monarch, dictator or head and the balance of the population servants or slaves.

America is no exception.

Since the early 60's America has been invaded with a—*spirit of moral decay*—one that engulfed the minds of this generation. Fifty years later we are paying the price for this spiritual decay of anti-God, anti-Christian and pro-everything that the Apostle Paul teaches about in Galatians chapter 5 verses 19-21 called the works of the flesh.

"Now the works of the flesh are manifest, which are these; adultery, fornication, uncleanness, lasciviousness, idolatry, witchcraft, hatred, variance, emulations, wrath, strife, seditions, heresies, envying, murders, drunkenness, and such like: of which I have also told you in they that do such things shall not inherit the kingdom of

God.

Is it any wonder that Paul tells us in Romans chapter 1 verse 28, *"And even as they did not retain God in their knowledge, God gave them over to a reprobate mind, to do those things which are not convenient."*

In order to understand this verse in its fullest meaning, we need to read the preceding verses.
Romans 1:20-32

"For the invisible things of him from the creation of the world are clearly seen, being understood by the things that are made, even his eternal power and God-head: so that they are without excuse.
21. "Because that, when they knew God, they glo-rified him not as God, neither were thankful, but became vain in their imaginations, and their foolish heart was darkened. 22. Professing themselves to be wise, they be-came fools. 23. And changed the glory of the uncorrupt-ible God into an image made like to corruptible man, and to birds, and four footed beasts, and creeping things.
24. Wherefore . . .
God also gave them up to uncleanness through the lusts of their own hearts, to dishonor their own bodies between themselves. 25. Who changed the truth of God into a lie and worshipped and served the creature more than the Creator, who is blessed for ever. Amen. 26. For this cause

God gave them up unto vile affections; for even their women did change the natural use into that which is against nature. 27. And likewise also the men, leaving the natural use of the woman, burned in their lust one toward another; men with men working that which is unseemly, and receiving in themselves that recompense of their error which was meet. 28. (see on previous page)

The Apostle Paul continues by naming the "lust of the flesh" in great detail in verses 29 to 32.

29. Being filled with all unrighteousness, sexual immorality, wickedness, covetousness, maliciousness; full of envy, murder, strife, deceit, evil mindedness; they whispers, 30. backbiters, haters of God, violent, proud, boasters inventors of evil, disobedient to parents, 31. undiscerning, untrustworthy, unloving, unforgiving, unmerciful; 32. who, knowing the righteous judgment of God that those who practice such things are deserving of death, not only do the same but also approve of those who practice them.

Read Galatians 5:19-21 — where the Apostle addresses this same issue...works of the flesh.

The President
Barack H. Obama
2008—2016

The roots of a tree determine its size, trunk, branches and the fruit it bears. Obama's roots dug deep in the ideology of Islam and the anti-colonialism hatred of the United Kingdom. This hatred fostered the mind set and encouraged the fight of his father to finally free the chains that bound his country to the United Kingdom.

This hatred, even as a young child, raised its ugly head as he was reared in a Muslim school for the first few years of his life and then later under the tutorage of his grandparents (his mother's mother and dad) who were devout socialist/communist had to hatch the eggs of anger and hatred. He sat at the feet of a known communist, Frank who is mentioned in one of his novels.

As a community organizer, he appeared to be well known for his liberal socialist mindset. In over twenty years, sitting under the ministry of Reverend Wright, he mentioned that he never heard any of the sermons, damming America or Wright's Black Liberation Theology.

On the campaign trail for President of the United States, he made statements about "hope and change" and in his second campaign, he used the word "Forward" which was later found to be used by the Nazi's.

Another thought to ponder: Why has the President taken so much pain, secrecy and millions of dollars to hide his birth certificate, passport, university aid for foreign students and his college grades or transcripts.

Famous quotes:

"Your health insurance will not increase. You will be able to keep your doctor. In fact you will save $2500.00 a year on insurance premiums."

"We need a National Civilian Force with as much financing as the Pentagon." - (does this sound like brown shirts in Germany)

"My administration will be the most transparent one in history."

"All these so called scandals are nothing more than 'phony' ways to get back at me, the President."

"We are no longer a Christian nation….we are a nation of Muslims and ————-

"Fort Hood Texas was a "work place violence, in the killing of our soldiers."

Presidential Czars*

A man is known by the company he keeps. Here's some of Obama's friends which were promoted by the President as Czars. Remember Czars are appointed by the President and Congress has no jurisdiction on approval or denial.

Czar: One that has great power of authority.

This power far exceeds any over sight by Congress nor questioned by Congress and thereby execute policy under the direction of the President.

Here's a list of some Czars from the year 2009 — appointed by President Obama.

Richard Holbrooke: Ultra liberal anti gun. Pro abortion and legal drug use.

Ed Montgomery: Black radical anti business activist. ACORN board member.

Jeffrey Crowley   Homosexual. Believes in gay marriage and special status.

Ron Bloom: Auto Union worker. Anti business and anti nuclear. Worked hard to force US auto makers out of business.

Carol Bower: Socialist on commission for Sustainable World Society which calls for 'global governance.'

Daniel Fried: Rights activist for Foreign Terrorists. Believes America has caused the war on terrorism.

George Mitchell: Left wing radical. Has advocated that Israel should be split up into 2 or 3 smaller manageable plots. Anti gun and pro homosexual.

John Holden: Fierce ideological environmentalist. Anti-business activist. Ok to abort a child until the age of two. Thinks trees should be able to sue humans. Limiting population growth.

John Brennan: Anti CIA activist. Suggest Obama disband US Military. Open borders to Mexico. RECENTLY appointed CIA director. Brennan (reported to have converted to Islam) and now is the CIA director.

Ashton Carter: Leftist. Wants all private weapons in US destroyed. Supports UN ban on firearms ownership in America.

Kevin Jennings: Safe School Czar—Wrote the intro to the book, "Queering Elementary Education." Supports Harry Hay of NAMBLA—North American Man

Boy Love Association. A homosexual in heart and practice. As a teacher he was having sex with an older man and instead of turning him in suggested they start using condoms. Held a conference with the MAXIMUM age of 18 to teach homosexual issues like 'fisting.'

Some of these people may have moved on to other positions in this administration or left to pursue private opportunities.

* This list was composed and printed in a Conservative Magazine.

Council on American
Islamic Relations—CAIR

CAIR—Council on American Islamic Relations sued in federal court by former clients that claimed CAIR defrauded them by failing to provide the legal services they had been promised. It was during this court case that the legal discovery showed money laundering by CAIR.

> *To avoid reporting these millions of dollars from the dubious Islamist sources and to avoid registering as an agent for a foreign country by federal law, CAIR created a separate organization, CAIR Foundation which was passed by IRS as a 501© (3) charitable organization. The result is that CAIR now receives millions of dollars from foreigners every year, but only has to report the amounts of its income as the funds are transferred to the Foundation.*

CAIR is the largest Muslim Brotherhood-Hamas front group in America. While they build themselves as a civil rights organization, they are an unindicted co-conspirator in the Holy Land Foundation criminal trial.

The largest terrorism finances prosecution to date, resulting in convictions of directors and board members with sentences of 20 to 65 years.

Due to the close relationship of this president and his administration with CAIR and the Brotherhood, the Department of Justice has failed to act in securing the safety of all Americans.

Loop holes:

1. That by-pass the security of America
2. American banks catering to Sharia Financing
3. American courts using Sharia Law to settle Muslim cases — not our Constitutional Laws
4. Extreme political correctness by our leaders
5. Allowing CAIR to fight our Constitutional rights in court — against using foreign or International laws

"Islam isn't in America to be equal to any other faith, but to become dominant."

"The Quran, the Muslim book of scriptures, should be the highest authority in America and Islam the only accepted religion on earth."

By the founder of Council of American-Islamic Relations

There is nothing 'moderate' about CAIR or Islam. In fact we have seen CAIR actively intimidate others to shut down talks by conservative authorities on the wiles and evil of Islam. We have seen them demand and get special privileges in public schools; prayer time, food accommadions and Imams teaching Muslim social studies.

We also see an administration that actively covers

for and diverts attention from this Islamic organization and others like it.

I recently viewed a documentary, "Jihad in America: The Grand Deception" which focuses on stealth jihadists and how they try to control public perception. Part of it is by manipulating a lazy and gullible media. CAIR is using the main line media as a cover by calling any out cry against Islam or Muslims as bigots, racist or Islamophobia. They shut down any criticism of Islamist ideology—the notion that society is best governed by Islamic Law—Sharia.

We are not to be confused by men wearing 3 button blue stripe or black suits holding up a Quran and crying we are a 'religion of peace.' The first part of the Qur'an talks about peace—but it is abrogated by the last part of the Qur'an which nullifies the first part—peaceful religion and presents a holy war against the infidels.

There was a reason for this. In the beginning the prophet came in the name of peace until he was able to build a large military presence to subdue his so called enemies or those that would not embrace his religion.

It was nearly 60 years after his death that the name Muslim came into existence. Does this mean that Islam is a made up religion by wicked men—and for men.

Beware the enemy is in our midst.

The Executive Director of CAIR, Dallas-Fort Worth, Texas in a recent speech told the Muslim group that "practicing Muslims loyal to Allah and the prophet (peace be upon him) are above the laws of the land.)"

A well known Congressman woman from Houston, Texas, who is one of the top ten recipients of Arab-Muslim money, advocates for CAIR at a fundraiser in 2007. She presented the CAIR organization a congressional recognition award and in her own words, "How proud I am to have been associated with CAIR."

The Los Angeles, California Congresswoman from the South Central LA district appeared in a Muslim community meeting along with the Los Angeles County Sheriff and the Deputy Assistant Police Chief of the Los Angeles Police Department. During this meeting, she advocated for CAIR and the Muslim community including a proclamation she made in Congress of the asset of the Muslim community.

The Assistant LA City Police Chief advocated for the Muslim community with a statement: "We have to listen to the Muslim community . . . "

The Sheriff of Los Angeles County laughs when CAIR is brought up in a conversation about them being a co-conspirator with the Holy Land Foundation trial. I quote; "If they have committed a crime I will pursue it." while smiling at the Muslim group. "What does this say?"

Anti-Islam
and not anti -Muslim

Islam is a religious, political, militaristic, economic and social ideology, but Muslims are people who adhere to the tenets of Islam. Many of them are ignorant of what Islam actually teaches. It is entirely possible to be anti-Islam without being anti-Muslim.

I am such a person.

There are moderate American Muslims who are enjoying the freedom and liberty that America affords under our Constitution, while others are using 'stealth jihad' to undermine the Constitution in favor of Sharia Law.

Some of these moderates are branded as traitors or apostates by the Muslim Brotherhood and many Sharia countries.

Others on this hate list are the following: Allen West, Pamela Geller, Robert Spencer and several Congress people plus other persons and organizations that understand the threat that true Islam is an ideology for world dominance. The world, under Allah and Sharia, enslaves people in all aspects of their life—family, social and legal.

Muslim Brotherhood
Government/School Infiltration

The Muslim Brotherhood's roots in America have expounded tremendously. Their mission statement gives us the insight of this parasite organization and its many sub roots.

Muslim Brotherhood in North America
FBI IDENTIFIED TERRORIST NETWORK IN OUR SCHOOLS AND COMMUNITIES   EducateUSA.org

Mountain View-Los Altos Union High School District club

Community College Clubs

University Clubs

SAAR Network

Council on American-Islamic Relations (CAIR)

Islamic African Relief Agency (IARA)

United Association for Studies and Research (UASR)

A.N.S.W.E.R.

Al Qaeda

Muslim Student's Association (MSA)

Holy Land Foundation (HLF) $$$

Islamic Circle of North America (ICNA)

Saudi Arabia

Islamic Association For Palestine (IAP)

World Assembly of Muslim Youth (WAMY)

Muslim Brotherhood

Hamas

The Mosque Foundation (MF)

Islamic Society of North America (ISNA)

$$$ Global Relief Foundation (GRF)

Muslim Youth of North America (MYNA)

North American Islamic Trust (NAIT)

Muslim World League (MWL)

Palestine Islamic Jihad (PIJ)

Muslim American Society (MAS)

American Muslim Council (AMC)

International Institute for Islamic Thought (IIIT)

040409MH
Partial representation of Muslim Brotherhood network compiled from Federal Terrorist Financing trial evidence presented against the Holy Land Foundation (HLF) in 2007

The Litmus Test
You're fired!

A Special Report from ABC
Evening News

There seems to be some credible evidence, that since last year and through this year, that there have been a 'litmus test' given to American Military Officers. The main point of the test—"Would you fire on an American Citizen?" If you said no, then as Mr. Trump would say, "you're fired."

It appears this President is planning a 'war on citizens' and against the United States and he is firing those in the Military brass that oppose this action. Here's a list of nine officers who retired or were fired by the President and there are close to 200 more officers fired.

General Carter Hamm, Rear Admiral Charles Gaouette, Major General Ralph Baker, Brigadier General Bryan Roberts, Major General Gegg A. Sturdevant, Major General Charles M.M. Gurganus, Lt. General David Holmes Huntoon Jr, Vice Admiral Tim Giardina and Major General Michael Carry.

"What is Obama's next move?

EPA
The Power and Abuse of the Environmental Protection Agency

Under this administration—the fight for climate change has taken on an ugly face. The President has listed this as one of the most important agendas of his presidency, even though hundreds of scientist deny the value that the President is placing on it. It appears to many of them as a fraud on the citizens of America. With the decline of the coal industry and his ability to create chaos with this fossil fuel, it appears that thousands of jobs will be eliminated.

The EPA—Environmental Protection Agency has upped the tab for many businesses.

Under California's law, the California Air Resources Board is directed to implement the Cap and Trade program The CARB chairman is appointed by the governor (and like the Presidents Czars) operate outside Legislative oversight. In California, small and medium businesses will not be able to compete with many larger companies that can (pollute) and offset this pollution by buying credits from other companies that pollute less.

Global Warming or now called Climate Change, as a scientific theory, has been discredited by over 30,000 scientists worldwide including nearly 10,000 PhD's who also dispute man-made pollution causes 'greenhouse gasses." The concepts that CO-2 or Methane gases are pollutants is also widely debated. There is no scientific consensus authenticating the belief.

Do you realize that CO-2 is produced by humans every time they exhale? Although Methane gas is produced naturally by cows and other farm animas, *there is now a TAX on those emissions.'*

What does this have to do with the citizens of California? These severe over regulations will cause California electric rates to skyrocket, gasoline and diesel fuel will increase and all deliverable goods will increase as the price of regulation will be passed on to the customer.

Now when you consider the President and his proposals for Cap and Trade—America will feel the same pain as those living in the 'golden (rusty) state.'

FEMA

In addition to many government agencies purchasing AK-15s, other guns and millions of rounds of ammo, FEMA has recently purchased 420 million survival meals, to keep them off the market for private citizens to purchase and store for their own survival.

It is a known fact that if you control the food and water supply you can control the people.

Why?

Why are there FEMA camps? Who will be enslaved in these camps without the protection of our Constitution.

"Islamophobia"
Radical Islam at its best

In the spirit of "the best defense, is a good offense." Accusations of Islamophobia were first slung broadly in this country to suppress attention to the Islamic Jihadist motivations of the perpetrators of the September 11th Twin Towers attack. CAIR and other organizations under the umbrella of the Muslim Brotherhood have used this tactic to slander or quiet those that threaten to expose the realities of the ideological basis of terrorism.

This type of accusations of Islamophobia have been used to silence or squelch European Politicians such as Geert Wilders, producer of the DVD "Fitna," which exposed the radical side of Islam in the Netherlands. High religious officers have called for Geert's death and he was charged by his own parliament for "hate speech" by producing and telling the truth in this DVD.

The psychological term phobia describes an excessive and irrational fear. This "fear" is appropriate willingness to heed the solid evidence of who commits terror acts and their motivations.

"Are all Muslims terrorist? NO."

"Are all terrorist Muslims? YES."

According to a study by the Justice department, while Muslims constitute about 1% of the American population, they contribute 80% of the Home Grown Terrorism. In other words, there is the probability of an American Muslim to conduct a terrorist act in the US 400 times the probability of American Non-Muslims to an act of terror. Since 9/11, there have been over 20,000 terrorist attacks in the world by Muslim jihadist.

In addition, the only nations that punishes or kils in our modern times for religious crimes, are Muslim states.

One of Sharia (Islamic) Law's central ideals which is approved by all the main schools of Islamic Jurisprudence—even to today—is declaring wars against Non-Muslims to spread Islam across the globe.

The practice of Sharia laws in Muslim countries consist of: killing apostates and sorcerers, hanging gays, honor killing, stoning adulterer women and using violence against women.

Where else in any religion will you find similar atrocities practiced in the name of religion other than — ISLAM.

Fear of Islam cannot be described as "Islamophbia" as this fear is based on facts and realities rather than irrationality as the word "phobia" would indicate. American concerns that religious teaching is the primary factor in contemporary terrorism must be heeded, not suppressed by name-calling tactics. Americans who allow themselves to be silenced by "Islamophobia" accusations serve as radical Islam's enablers.

Fear from Islam can only be changed when the MUSLIM world challenges itself to change the above mentioned frightening facts and realities.

Ask yourself this question?

Why would CAIR fight in our courts against using American Laws for American Courts. Are they prone to desire and want to use foreign, international or Sharia law in our court decisions.

Tenets of Sharia Law

Examples of Sharia Law include the following:*

> Requirement of women to obtain permission from husband's for daily freedoms.
> Beating of disobedient woman and girls.
> Execution of homosexuals.
> Polygamy and forced child marriages.
> Requirement of the testimony of four male witnesses to prove rape.
> Stoning of adulteresses.
> Lashing of adulterers.
> Amputation of body for criminal offenses.
> Female genital mutilation.
> Capital punishment for those who slander or insult Islam or the prophet.
> Execution of apostates or those that leave the religion of Islam.
> Inferior status for all non-Muslims known as dhimmitude.
> Concept of Taquiyya: A Muslim may lie or deceive others to advance the cause of Islam.

* The authoritative source, *"Reliance of the Traveler— The Sacred Manual of Islamic Law and the Life and Times of Muhammad.*

"Don't Let Your Kids Drink The Kool-Aid"
What are they teaching my kids in school?
Whitewash of Islam
Common Core

*Christianity was started by a young
Palestinian named Jesus.*

The 9/11 murderers were not Islamic Fundamentalist, but simply a generic "team of terrorist" that flew airplanes into the World Trade Center and other places killing both Muslims and other people.

Islam is treated with special "white gloves" and "gentle" handling of text with special privilege not afforded Judaism and Christianity. In the glossary of *World History: Continuity and Change:*

It calls the Ten Commandments "moral laws Moses CLAIMED to have received from the Hebrew God," while the entry for the Koran contains no such qualifier in saying it is the "Holy Book of Islam containing REVELATIONS received by Muhammad from God."

In the history book: *World History: The Modern World* intentionally leaves out the religion of the 9/11 hijackers. No mention of Islamic Fundamentalist. No mention of jihad. No attempt to explain the identities or murderous motivations of the madmen who perpetrated the most horrific attack on our country.

In the book, *History Alive! The Medieval World and Beyond* teaches students about the subject: Jihad.

"Jihad is defined as a struggle within each individual to overcome difficulties and strive to please god. Sometimes it may be a physical struggle for protection against enemies,"—the book reads, noting that Islam teaches "that Muslims should fulfill jihad with the HEART, TONGUE and HAND. Muslims use the heart in their struggle to resist evil."

Of course, there's no suggestion of what those hands might do should the heart and tongue fail to resolve the struggle. Nor that some of those hands held long gutted knives to slowly behead "infidels" (who are unbelievers of Islam) or to press the button of a suicide bomb to kill as many infidels as possible.

Nowhere does it teach the early history of Muhammad who in one of his battles killed 800 Jewish men and took their wives and children as slaves.

Neither does it instruct our children that Muhammad the prophet married a six year old and consummated when she was 9 and because he is the perfect example of a Muslim man, many old men marry young girls—some even babies—so now more than ever, parents need to get involved in their children's education, by monitoring school books and stand up and scream at school boards and superintendents should we discover any ideology that is abusive or in error.

In *Ways of the World,* Christians and Muslims share with the Jews the hope of a better world where Good triumphs over Evil." While the Koran states, 'good' as defined with Islam ruling the political and religious world. In the Hadith, Bukhari reports that Muhammed said that "the entire world must become a place for Islam."

In *Ways of the World*, "Islamic Civilizations have a long history of encouraging religious tolerance and guaranteeing the rights of religious minorities."

Question: "If Islam is so tolerant, how did Turkey, Egypt, North Africa, Syria and Iraq go from being Christian to Islamic? The rights of a religious minority were limited to being a dhimmi, a semi-slave without citizen rights.

History Alive! The Medieval World and Beyond covers history from the fall of Rome to the Enlightenment. Quite properly, the book gives more space to Western history and culture as the principal source of American civilization. Fourteen of its 35 chapters address the legacy of Rome, European feudalism, the growth of towns, the Byzantine Empire, the Renaissance, the Reformation, the age of exploration and the scientific revolution. Other units treat the culture and kingdoms of West Africa 3 chapters), imperial China (4 chapters), medieval Japan (3 chapters), and the pre-Columbian civilizations of the

America (5 chapters).

What will distain us, the unit on *The Rise of Islam*," noteworthy because it provides several varieties of detail no other strand of world history receives. Its 5 chapters cover the geography of Arabia, the life of the religion's founder, the teachings of Islam, the contributions of Muslims to world civilization, and the Crusades and the Spanish re-conquest.

Strange for a book of medieval history, there are seven photographs of Muslims engaged in religious observance today, strongly hinting at its real agenda: to depict Islam as unchanging over time, in line with the beliefs and aims of Islamist ideologues.

There is a full chapter on the person, called the prophet, Muhammad. When you search further, there is no chapter, paragraph or evidence on the life of Jesus, except this: "Christians are followers of Jesus, who, according to Christian Scripture, was put to death on a Roman cross in the first century c.e."

Much more objectionable material is on display in the chapter entitled, *The Teachings of Islam.* NOTE: this has nothing to do with history but another way of whitewashing Islam and making it sound like it is the "religion of peace."

Proproganda— If you visited any city in a Sharia or Muslim country today, you would notice many things that reflect the teachings of Islam. Five (5) times a day, would hear a call to prayer throughout the city. You would see people dressed modestly, and many women wearing a head scarf. You would find that Muslims do not drink alcohol or eat pork. You might learn how Muslims give money to support their houses of worship and practiced as a complete way of life.

Saudi in the classroom:

The Stealth Curriculum: Manipulating America's History Teachers, by offering Harvard's outreach training programs for K-12, designed "whitewashing" treatments of the life and teachings of Muhammad and the "revelation" and spread of Islam, with exercises calling on students to "appoint imams," memorize Islamic principles, and act out prayer at a mosque.

This notebook claims Muslims beat Columbus to the New World supposedly sailing the Atlantic in 880. It also includes viewing "the history of freedom as the history of oppression" and urging students "to be more sympathetic to cultures that don't value individual rights than to those that do."

This proproganda is sold directly to schools or teachers, thereby bypassing public scrutiny.

Does this sound like history?

The history teacher, in a local middle school in Southern California, said — "each of the students picked a Muslim name, but she didn't address them in class by the

name. The students learned the five (5) pillars of Islam —
because the State of California mandates that all 7th grad-
ers learn them. (Note: What about the Lord's prayer...this
is a no, no — for ACLU would sue). The students could
dress up in Muslims robes to earn extra points for a play
they were asked to put on. Also, students could give up
watching television or fast lunch during Ramadan.

A Texas group of citizens, reading and studying
American and World History books that are being taught
in our school class, found over 1500 errors.

In other words, our students are learning false information, especially about our foundering fathers, the
revolution and our Constitution.

Common Core
Federal Take Over of our Schools

What is Common Core?

Common Core is a federally funded standard of education standards to curriculum. Each state will receive federal funds when they sign up and address this in the school districts. It is designed as a standard not only for the US but applies to the world and seems to be monitored by the United Nations.

1. Common Core war on math standards:

Under CC, algebra I instruction is pushed to 9th grade instead of 8th grade as commonly taught. Division is postponed from 5th to 6th grade. Prime factorization, common denominators, conversions of fractions and decimals and algebraic manipulation are de-emphasized or eschewed. Tradition Euclidean geometry is replaced with an experiment approach that had not been previously pilot-tested in the US.

2. Common Core's deconstruction of English and literature.

The new achievement goals will actually set American students back by de-emphasizing great literary works for "informational texts." Challenging students to digest and dissect difficult poems and novels is becoming passé.

The CC criteria call for students to spend only half of their class time studying literature and only 30 percent of their class time by their junior and senior years in high school.

Under CC, classics such as "To Kill a Mockingbird" and "The Adventures of Huckleberry Finn" are of no more academic value than the pages of the Federal Register. This CC standard allows for more culture themes of today, such as pop song lyrics, RAP and other music on par with Shakespeare.

English professor Mary Grabar describes CC training exercises that tell teachers *"to read Lincoln's Gettysburg Address without emotion and without providing any historical context."*

3. Common Core's mindless political correctness: The dirty secret of why—progressive activists reign supreme in government schools. Having been taught by socialist/communist professors in college or our elite universities, they have succumbed to this brainwashing.

This is why in a red state like Texas, a high school geography teacher could incite and instruct students in the study of Islam would ban them from using the words "suicide bomber" and "terrorist" to describe Muslim mass murderers in favor of the term "freedom fighter."

How about teaching students that the Boston Tea Party participants were "terrorist."

4. Common Core's invasive student tracking database.

These systems will aggregate massive amounts of personal data—healthcare histories, income information, religious affiliations, voting status and even blood types and homework completion. This data will be available to a wide variety of public agencies.

It is imperative that parents in America be familiar with Common Core's different functions and how it affects your children's education.

My granddaughter under Common Core has been held back from excelling in school so as not to damage the egos of some students that are not up to par.

California at the present time has a grade of D+ in math and English according to a recent study. The State is 47th in education according to this study. Find out where your state ranks and fight the system of complacency.

This is just the tip of the iceberg of what is Common Core?

Children morphed into human capital— tracking children by blood type, birth marks, eye color and more.

Under Common Core, teachers and children are classified as 'Human Capital" under CCIS. Instead of a Human Resource Department, it will change to Strategic Management of Human Capital.

"What does this mean?"

Your child becomes "Human Capital" to enter the workforce. This program places your child into two basic categories: K-12 educational with emphasis on secondary (those that qualify for college) and the balance in the labor/workforce system.

The purpose of Common Core or better yet, Human Capital is to allow policymakers a complete data base on each child which will allow them to look comprehensively at the stock and flow of Human Capital (your child) which is essential for effective planning in the globalized knowledge economy.

Common Core, a United Nations concept, promotes an even playing field. This means lowering American standards to meet those of the rest of the world. According to the UN the International salary average is $21,500. No cars, no air conditioning, no single family homes according to the United Nations Biodiversity.

Human Capital is taught that private property must take a backseat for the good of the collective. (Do you smell socialism/communism in this statement/agenda.) The students (Human Capital) should go to college, accumulate massive debt estimated at over one trillion. Debt will be so massive that marriage, home or car ownership will be unattainable or uture generations.. CC teaches collectivism, that one shoe fits all, which is the antithesis of individual greatness.

American values and free market economics are not taught under CCIS. Students (Human Capitals) are taught to rely on the government. Only collectivism through social justice is part of the training — when today over 50% of Human Capitals think it is the governments job to take care of them.

Our American and World history books are a sham. They are not being taught American history from the beginning of our Republic and the sacrifices made our foundering fathers, neither are they being instructed on the true agenda of Islam. The history books "white-wash" Islam and Muhammad—as a religion of peace when in reality it is composed of, military, political, social and last of all religion.

According to a Florida Republican Party email—CCIS is a venture capitalist's dream. Follow the money:

This program was created and endorsed by the vendors, extremely wealthy elitist—Bill Gates Foundation invested 354 millions dollars—in conjunction with the United Nations, who will benefit the most from the program.

Under Obama's administration, Obama used blackmail to entice the states to adopt Common Core. The Educational Department would not release any RTTT federal funds to those states that refused to adopt and use Common Core

Common Core was designed so that it is outside the legislative control and that CCIS dictates the curriculum. CC is a simple way of brainwashing our children, from (pre-kindergarten to K-12 and beyond.

Common Core and Agenda 21 are twins in destroying America and our 'free spirit' and 'capitalism'.

Then there's APUSH*—AP U.S. History curriculum, a melting down of American history.

APUSH is new. It came into existence quite recently under dubious and secretive circumstances (just like Common Core). If fully implemented, APUSH would greatly modify and standardize the teaching of US History in every high school.

APUSH fits right with Common Core and a one size fits all curriculum. It rejects the history that has been taught in the country for generations. It has an emphasis on race, gender, class, ethnicity, grievance and American bashing while simultaneously omitting the most basic structural and philosophical elements considered essential to the understanding of American History for generations.

APUSH omits the following: Jefferson, Adams, Madison, Franklin and not even a mention of Martin Luther King, Jr. who was on the forefront of the civil rights movement. It ignores lessons on the Boston Tea Party, Lexington, Jefferson's First Inaugural Address, and Lincoln's Gettysburg Address.

Like Common Core, we must reject these progressive (sponsored by the United Nations) and now APUSH ideas. They are your children. Fight for them, as they do not have a voice in the matter.

*Heartland.org/newspaper-article

Never Forget
9/11

It matters not what a president says, about the so called *religion of peace,* "We are not at war with Islam."

This is a complete 'bogus' statement.

Since 9/11 there have been over 20,000 jihadist attacks world wide. America has suffered minor damage from these attacks, but we are not completely immune as there are 'Homegrown Terrorist Camps' and 'sleeper cells' abiding their time to strike fear in the hearts of Americans.

We are aware of at least 30 Homegrown Terrorist Camps spread throughout America. There may be some in your state. It behooves you to find the answers and quickly recognize that we are at "war with Islam."

Time has a way of subduing our thinking process. We are bombarded with liberal media and politicians that encourage the Muslim population to use political correctness as a means of by-passing or converting our Constitution.

We Will Never Forget!

We will never forget!

Christianity vs. Islam

One of the principles of ISIS or now called the Islamic State is that Muslims must fight non-Muslins all over the world (including the great Satan—America) and follow Muhammad's life of offering them three choices: *1. Convert to Islam, 2. Pay a humiliating tax, (jizya) or 3. to be killed. Not very pretty choices for a Kafir.*

This violent principle, set by Muhammad, was the basic doctrine that justified the Islamic conquests of Christian countries throughout Europe and Africa during the early stages of Islam.

After the recent demonic mindset by ISIS and other militant groups, the following question is raised. "Is it possible to be a follower and not adhere to that mandate?"

Like a young Christian that adheres to the Words of the Bible (New Testament) and follows in the footpaths of Jesus teachings to evangelize the world through love, compassion and acceptance, is there any other source that contradicts this teachings.

Is there any other (abrogation) record that voids or nullifies this teaching? Absolutely not!

Now, apply this same principle to a young Muslim who follows the footpath of Muhammad, the Koran and the Hadith, is there any other source or interpretation that contradicts such a principle as killing the Kafir-non-Muslim. NO!

Islamic Law: Better known as Sharia derives it source from the Koran, the Hadith of Prophet Muhammad, the actions of the disciples of Muhammad, the four schools of Islamic jurisprudence, and the Tafseer or Interpretations of the Koran.

Adhering to the complete doctrine of Islam, you would feel the shocking results —

Koran 9:29 can easily be used to justify what extremists are doing. *"Fight those who do not believe in Allah or in the Last Day and who do not consider unlawful what Allah and His Messenger have made unlawful and who do not adopt the religion of truth from those who were given the Scripture (Jews and Christians)-(fight) until they give the jizya willingly while they are humiliated."*

In the Hadith in Al-Buchakry also supports violent ideology. "Muhammad said: *"I have been ordered to fight the people till they say; (none has the right to be worshipped but Allah), and whoever said No God other than, Allah will save his property and his life from me."*

The fourth source of Islamic law is the four schools of Islamic jurisprudence, these schools support the principle that Muslims must fight non-Muslims and offer them the dire choices-convert, taxes and humiliation or death.

Is there a way around this verse in the Koran for anyone that searches for a different understanding or interpretation that states it different?

A basic search of all approved (note approved) interpretation for the Koran supports the same violent understanding.

Saying that "Islam is the religion of peace," as stated by President Bush, or as President Obama stated in his address to the citizens of America, *"let's make two things clear, ISIL is not Islamic. NO RELIGION condones the killing of innocents, and the vast majority of ISIL's victims have been Muslim."*

What our leaders fail to acknowledge, the fact remains that Islam is at WAR with America and all free people of the world. They must condemn the principle that Muslims must fight non-Muslims to subjugate them to Islam.

Our leaders, those in power that are non-Muslim, will endure the same fate as other free loving people of the world — convert, tax and humiliation or death.

So when our President (who I believe knows exactly what he is doing in abetting the enemy) and all of our leaders hide their head in the sand of "political correctness," a great price will be paid.

It is dangerously evident when we fail to use the terms in describing the enemy: Islam, Islamic, Terrorist, Muslims, Sharia or any other name that denotes the effects of Islam, then the enemy of America has won one part of the war.

When CAIR—Counsel for American Islamic Relations, uses our court system to push law suits, against American Laws for American Courts; it shows their true identity as un-American citizens. Who in their right mind, except Muslims, would want to be judged by Sharia Law or any other foreign law, by-passing our own Constitution.

GLOSSARY

Caliph—Title of Islamic supreme leader

Dar-al-Islam—Regions of people under Islamic rule. Lands of submission and/or peace.

Dawa— Muslim missionary efforts to convert non-believers.

Dhimmi—The inferior second-class status of non-Muslims.

Halal—Sharia approved. Can be applied to food, banking or any Shaia approved activity.

Haram—Forbidden. Criticisms or questioning of Islam is considered haram, as is any expression of free thought.

Imam—Spiritual leader of a mosque.

Innocent—According to Islam only Muslims can be innocent.

Islam—Submission or resignation. "Peace," The Islamic definition of peace refers to the protection of the nation of Islam, and the conversion of all infidels or non-Muslims.

Jihad—Struggle with the temptations of life and the struggle to wage war against all infidels by any and all means necessary.

Kafir—A soiled or dirty person, any non-Muslim.

Glossary cont.

Mujahideen—An Islamic warrior

Shiat—Muslims who believe that Ali, Muhammad's cousin and son-in-law was the first Imam.

Sunni—Almost 85% of the world's Muslims are Sunni, believing that Abu Bakr was the first Imam.

Taqiyyah—The permission to lie either by omission or commission in order to protect or advance Islam.

>>>>

Holy Land Foundation Trial

The 2007 trial of the Holy Land Foundation for Relief and Development, the largest Muslim charity in North America, which supplied money and assistance to Hamas for terrorist activities.

Many of their top leaders are in prison.

CAIR– Council for American Islamic Relations was listed as a co-conspirator during this trial. According to reliable sources President Obama and his Attorney General, Eric Holder would not pursue these charges against CAIR and their leaders.

"Islamic Terror"

Right now there are only two major terrorist groups, Islam State and Al Quaeda, that demand media attention. However, all over the world, radical jihadist organizations are committing acts of terror—killings, beheadings, kidnapping, rape and forced marriages.

Look at these names:

Boko Haram	al-Nusrah Front	Hamas
Hezbollah	Army of Islam	Ansaru
Ansar Dine	Mujahidin Shura Council in the Environs of Jerusalem	
Ansar Bayt al-Maqdis	Ansar al-Sharia in Benghazi	
The Muslim Brotherhood	Abu Sayyaf	
The Haqqani network		

And under the Muslim Brotherhood in America, there are a host of organizations that promote 'stealth jihad' in our political arena, federal, state, county and city government.

>>>>

The stated goal of radicals, moderates or stealth jihad is to establish an Islamic Caliphate which will be governed by a single supreme religious Islamic leader.

Anyone not willing to convert to the form of Islam, practiced by Muslims, will be either killed or subdued as second class citizens and pay the jizya (tax) to live and serve Muslims.

It appears not to be a big or good choice as a Christian. Convert, live or die.

"Muslims must understand that all their work in America is a kind of grand jihad in eliminating and destroying America from within.

Obama and the Islamic State
How Obama, Bush & Clinton helped create this monster.

Over ten (10) years ago, the Islamic State and the Caliphate were foretold—in striking detail by an al-Qaeda insider.

In August 2005, Spiegel Online International published an article by Yassin Musharbash, *"The Future of Terrorism: What al-Qaeda Really Wants.*

This was a review of a book written by Fouad Hussein, a Jordanian journalist with close access to al-Qaeda and its affiliates, including the late Abu al-Zarqawi.

In the introduction of his book *Al Zarqawl: Al Quaeda's Second Generation:* Hussein interviewed different members with different ideologies, but with same agenda — war against America — the Great Satan and future conflicts.

Is a Caliphate in our future?

Read the balance of this story at your own risk or let it prepare you for what the future holds for America. It will seem impossible and infeasible, but keep in mind that under this administration (and the last two administrations, Bush and Clinton) that anything is possible when our national security is compromised.

There's seven (7) phases of the al-Qaeda's master plan as presented in Musharbash's 10 year old article.

The First Phase:

"The Awakening" — with the start of 9/11/2001 terrorist attacks, Washington played poker with the terrorist and the Islamic world, thereby "awakening Muslims. by invading the Middle East and fighting on their turf.

This first phrase was judged by the masterminds as very successful. Much of this makes sense, due to the "political correctness" of our leaders and media.

A few years after the Islamic strike on the World Towers, Americans elected a man with a Muslim name and upbringing and heritage for president. He continuously empowers the enemy — including (banning knowledge of Islam—the same ideology behind the strikes of 9/11. Later, he removed the words jihad, terrorist and radical from our law enforcement — even calling the Fort Hood killings, "workplace violence," instead of terrorism.

So, in phrase one — the poker hand went to the Muslims, 2000 to 2003.

The Second Phase:

"Opening Eyes" — according to Hussein's definition, the period we are now in — (2004-2005) and should last until 2006. Hussein says the terrorist hope to make the western conspiracy a "wake up call" for the Islamic community. He states that al-Qaeda wants the community to

develop into a movement, a network banking on recruiting young men during the Iraq invasion, that will be the center for all global operations.

This too is accurate (as prophecy seems to validate) at what is happening in the Middle East and in Western countries. The Islamic community, the umma, began to be more visible during this time frame, including through a rash of attacks and riots following any perceived "insult" to Islam.

With only 1% of the population in America, we see the handwriting on the wall as CAIR and the Muslim Brotherhood stretch their tentacles far and wide — with "political correctness" as one of their demands.

Due to a commander in chief, that favors and caters to the Muslim world, we are forbidden to say or speak the words, "terrorist," "jihad," — America is swiftly falling in the abyss, with a possibility of no return.

The Third Phase:

"Arising and Standing Up"— and should last from 2007 to 2010 and will be a focus on Syria, prophesies Hussein, based on what his sources told him. This uprising will extend from Syria (with the help of Obama supplying weapons — which are now used by the IS) to Iraq and more explosive attacks are planned in the region to establish a "caliphate."

Obama is complicit to this uprising, when he was warned that leaving Iraq would create a vacuum and leave the country open and ripe for ISIL to pick up the spoils.

The Fourth Phase:

Between 2010 and 2013, Hussein writes that al-Qaeda will aim to bring a total collapse of the hated Arabic governments. The estimate is that "the creeping loss of the regimes will to a steady growth in strength within al-Qaeda. At the same time attacks will be carried out on suppliers and the US economy will be targeted using cyber terrorism.

Note: The timeline (2010 to 2013) coincides remarkably well with "Arab Spring," which culminated with Islamic terrorists and their allies taking over the leadership of several Muslim countries formerly ruled by secularized autocrats.

What part did Obama and this administration play in empowering the jihadist, (Egypt, Libya, Syria). By promoting the destruction and overthrow of these governments, Obama played (by consent) into the hands of the terrorist.

The Fifth Phase:

Between 2013 and 2016, this phase will usher in an Islamic state or caliphate and Western influence in the Islamic world will be null and void and with Israel weakened so much, that resistance will not be feared. Al-Qaeda hopes that by then the Islamic State will be able to usher in a *New World Order.*

What happened in 2014, the Islamic State declared itself the caliphate, with many Muslim organization around the world pledging their allegiance.

This present administration helped empower jihadis during April Spring and in the name of "democracy" in Egypt, Libya and Syria, it helped the creation of the Islamic State by withdrawing US military forces that were keeping al-Qaeda at bay in Iraq.

As commander in chief, Obama continue to withdraw our troops, against the advice of his leaders, leaving the area wide open for the enemy and their master plan to unfold and create the caliphate.

The Sixth Phase:

"Total confrontation" — from 2016 onwards there will be a total confrontation as the caliphate has been declared the "Islamic Army." It will instigate the "fight between the believers, the apostates and the non-believers.

"Who are the "apostates?"

The Islamic State made it clear, the declared war on and jihad on "those that have left Islam," including "hypocrites, meaning all Arab leaders that lean outside the box of Islam and the Muslim populations that are insufficiently Islam.

For this reason, the new caliph took on the name of "Au Bakr" — the name o the first historic caliph (who brought back into the fold of Islam all those Arabs who broke away after Muhammad died.**

The great conquest or jihad against neighboring infidels took place after all the Arab tribes were unified.

** *After the prophet of Islam died, a great number of Arabian tribes that had submitted to his rule by becoming Muslims — thought they could renege, and so they apostatized in droves. This sparked the first Ridda, or "apostasy wars," waged by Abu Bakr al-Sadiq, who became the first caliph on Muhammad's death in 632..*

For nearly two years, till his own death in 634, the caliphates entire energy was focused on waging jihad on all the recalcitrant Arab tribes, forcing them by the edge of the sword to return to the fold of Islam.

Tens of thousands of Arabs were burned, beheaded, dismembered or crucified in the process, according to Islamic history. Following in the footsteps of Abu Bakr, Islamic State is doing the same burning, beheading, and crucifixions. This mind set does not look good for the "moderates" of Islam and even those that oppose the Islamic State and desire for a better world than what Sharia offers.

The Seventh Phase:

"Definitive victory" — This phrase remains to be seen, as it has another five years to go. With our Western leaders sticking their heads in the sand or drawing a fictitious "red line," it makes one to wonder if they are capable or have the stomach and guts to fight against this enemy of demonic beings.

Hussein writes that in their eyes, the rest of the world will be so beaten down by the 1 1/2 billion jihadist, the caliphate will undoubtedly succeed.

This phrase should be completed by 2020.

NOTE:

This is all well and good for the Muslims, however, Hussein forgot to mention that Jehovah—The Almighty God — is still in charge of this universe.

As a Christian writer, America is destined to feel the pain and torture that a **God—less—Nation** will reap what we have sown over the years, in our moral decline and forsaking the promises and benefits of God.

As the writer in scripture so aptly states:

"Look up for your redemption draws nigh."

Apostate—the penalty of death!

Islam's war on the apostate, so little known in the West, figures prominently in Islamic history. Indeed, Sheikh Yusuf al-Qaradawi, one of the most influential Islamic clerics today, while once discussing the importance of KILLING any Muslim who apostatizes from Islam on Al Jazeera, correctly stated that *"If the (DEATH) penalty for apostasy was ignored, there would NOT BE an Islam today.*

Islam would have ended on the death of the prophet, Muhammad.

>>>>

The Islamic State argues that the first and greatest enemy of Islam—the nearest enemy— is the *apostate* and the *hypocrite,* for they are the most capable of subverting Islam from within.

Executing Muslims

Democracy in America:

Author Alexis deTocqueville penned these words in his book, *Democracy in America.* "When I first came to America from France (1831), the religious aspect of the country was the first thing that struck my attention; and the longer I stayed there, the more I perceived the great political consequences resulting from this new state of things. In France I had almost always seen the spirit of religion and the spirit of freedom marching in opposite directions. But in America I found they were united and that they reigned in common over the same country."

He continued:

"Not until I went into some of America's churches and heard her pulpits flame with righteousness did I understand the secret of her genius and power. *America is great because America is good, and if America ever ceases to be good, America will cease to be great.*"

Was this statement, prophecy — of the decline of morals and inept social preaching in the pulpits of America's churches today? Is this the day that God talks about in Isaiah 56:10-11? *"His watchmen are blind, they are all ignorant; they are all dumb dogs; they cannot bark. Sleeping, lying down, and loving to slumber. Yes, they are greedy dogs, Which never have*

enough. And they are shepherds, Who can not understand;
They all look to their own way, Every one for his own
gain, From his own territory.

The author was recently invited to speak at an Aglow International meeting. I was asked to address three things: "Don't let your kids drink the Kool-Aid, Common Core and the threat of Islam in our schools.

My first question to this group:

"Is the Church responsible for the turmoil, corruption and moral decay in America today?"

YES, Without a clear message declaring the Word in its fullest content and meaning, as the inspired Word of God, we have failed in our responsibility to our members and the citizens outside the four walls of our church.

YES, We are voiceless when Muslim children can pray in school, during classes, and Christians fail to voice their opinions.

YES, We are voiceless when our sons and daughters are taught the tenets of Islam, dress as Muslims and pray as Muslims — while attending school.

YES, We have allowed liberal ministers to speak for us—on social, gay and political agendas

YES, We have allowed some scriptures to confuse us, as ministers, of getting involved in the political arena. We cater to Romans 13, but fail to realize we are to render unto God the things that are His. If we fail in this world to reach the lost, what good is heaven in the by and by.

YES, When we fail to vote, we are guilty of

allowing the enemy to vote for us. Is this why we have corruption in high places?

We are in a spiritual battle, thus we need to stand our ground. Realizing that God is on our side, He encourages us to stand still and see the salvation of the Lord.

We are in a spiritual and cultural battle!

If we don't win the cultural battle for our children's minds and hearts, they will not have a future at all.
.   When we are lax or dismiss the propaganda of the media, public schools, universities and churches as not relevant, then we have surrendered our kids to the welfare of the government.

Mark Dice interviewed ten universities students and asked the question: "Who causes more trouble in the world — ISIS or America?
The students are political science majors, answered—
AMERICA!

Most of America's pulpits are filled with cowardly men or social liberal men and women who are a shame of the Christ they claim to serve.

What is the cause of these timid leaders?

They have succumbed to political correctness— being brainwashed in liberal theology at our universities.
Our preachers are using self-help books and stories to supplement the Bible or preaching dead men's sermons, fiddling while the nation burns.
A minister worth his salt is branded as too harsh, judgmental or we are not "called" to fight evil, that's God's battle. Besides God loves everyone, regardless of

their lifestyle and there's more than one way to heaven.

What we need today is the thundering voices of men like Luther, Calvin, Wigglesworth and Knox. We need the voice of Jonathan Edwards preaching, "Sinners in the Hands of an Angry God." We need another Billy Graham or a Martin Luther King.

"Without a vision, the people perish."

While our nation is killing babies, our schools are indoctrinating Christian kids in Secular Humanism and Islam, "the religion of peace," where they learn the tenets of Islam.

When America began to forsake the founding fathers foundation of our Constitution, God slowly began to remove his hand of protection and allowed the enemy (just like Israel when they rebelled against God) to come to destroy and take men captive.

Frightening percentage of our kids believe that:
> Socialism is better than free market
> Christianity is judgmental and just mean
> America is the villain of world history
> Family does not mean marriage
> Human greed (climate change) is destroying the earth
> Of course, we need the government to take care of us

What does this say or tell us.

"The Kids are drinking the Kool-Aid"

Public schools are destroying the faith of Christian children. Legislation is introduced to remove the rights of parents. Children are taught they came from apes.

Precious babies are being murdered in the womb. Judges make laws and twist the Constitution. Tolerance trumps truth. Homosexual sodomy is granted legal protection. The institution of marriage is a thing of the past.

Great civilizations of the past (recorded in the Bible and History verifies) have gone to a watery grave.

Just like the Titanic, the ship that even God couldn't sink, sunk to a watery grave.

Can we stop this deluge——

It will take a miracle. The beliefs and values that once served as the foundation for our government and the moral compass for our society already have been so under minded among our youth that it will take a MIRACLE to restore them.

God is the answer:

II Chronicles 7:14 "If my people who are call by my name will humble themselves, pray and seek my face, then will I hear from heaven…

Winston Churchill:

"If you will not fight for right when you can easily win without bloodshed, if you will not fight when your victory is sure and not too costly, you may come to the moment when you will have to fight with all the odds against you and only a precarious chance of survival. There may even be a worse case. You may have to fight when there is no hope of victory, because it is better to perish than to live as slaves."

Remember the words of Patrick Henry!
"Give me liberty or give me death."

Ring of Fire:
The Revolution:

The battle cry in 1776 by Patrick Henry still rings volumes to patriots today, *"Is life so dear, or peace so sweet, as to be purchased at the price of chains and slavery? Forbid it, Almighty God! I know not what course others may take, but as for me, give me liberty, or give me death!"*

To The Infidel World

Jews News Report:

This article was written by an ex-Muslim and appeared in the Jews News on November 10, 2014. It is a subject that will affect America, Western Civilization and the balance of the world.

I was born and raised as a Muslim. I left Islam when I read the Koran and some of the books on Muhammad and knew in my heart that Islam is a sick and evil religion. In the mind of IS and all those that follow IS and the letter of the law — Koran, there is a message for the West.

1. The constitution for the new Islamic Republic or EU and USA are under construction.
2. We fill fight the infidel to death. We love death more than the infidel loves life.
3. American Laws and Constitution protects us.
4. Democrats and leftist will support us.
5. United Nations will legitimize us.
6. CAIR will incubate us.
7. ACLU will empower us.
8. Western Universities will educate us.
9. Mosque will shelter us.
10. Hollywood will love us.

11. OPEC will finance us.
12. Our children will attend the largest universities as exchange students and you the taxpayers pay.
13. We will use your "welfare system."
14. We will take advantage of your kindness, compassion and political correctness and "fear."
15. We will lie on camera and to your politicians and teach our children something different at home. We are Muslims, with the intent of ruling the world for Allah, and there's not anything you can do about it. Time is on our side.

When we are interviewed by the major networks, we will always say, "Islam is the religion of peace." In accord with our teaching, we will also say, "jihad" is an inner struggle — to please Allah.

We have brainwashed the "moderate Muslims" to tell your leaders, "There is no link between Islam (the religion of peace) and terrorism and the West will believe it.

We have many Muslim Brotherhood operatives in the White House, in many cabinet possessions, and it is just a matter of time before your "house of cards" dies from within.

We are deceivers: We may be your next door neighbor, coworker, student, teacher, professionals and you may even like us. You will find us well mannered, humble, and polite. BUT, we are still Muslims.

There's only one answer for America. It is found in II Chronicles chapter 7 verse 14. (read it in your Bible)

In these moments of despair, God will discipline us (sometimes with grievous punishment, we have never witnessed before, until 9/11) so we can be over comers and "the light set on a hill."

There is a passage in the Old Testament which talks about failures and restoration from God's perspective: Zephaniah 3:14-20.

Zephaniah was an interesting prophet and was of royal lineage, related to Hezekiah, one of the greatest Kings of God's people. Zephaniah wrote in the early 600's BC, that it was a time of great corruption among God's people. They worshipped idols, were unjust, greedy and Godless.

Zephaniah wrote to warn the people that God would not allow this to continue for long and that they would be disciplined if they continue in their sins and corruption.

During this period of time in history, the people had other prophets — Jeremiah, Nahum and Habakkuk — warning them of the same thing — judgment is coming.

Like most Old Testament prophets, there was a sense of hope — promises of forgiveness, redemption and restoration. God wanted his people to change before something terrible happened to them.

Thus, God is calling America to a place or repentance. If we are to escape the calamity and judgment of a righteous God, today is the time.

Why wonder in the wilderness of despair, depression and anguish when God's promises are for you as an individual and all of us as a nation to call on Him.

"Behold His hand is not shorten that it cannot save, neither is His ear heavy that He cannot hear."

The real revolution starts in the hearts of men and women, who desire and attest for real "hope" and "change," allowing the God of the universe to change us from the inside — out.

Daddy, when did America fail?

Michael, Devin and Nancy

A seven year old, looked up at his father, as they stood watching the 4th of July parade, *"daddy, when did America fail?"*

His father, stunned by the question, stared in space, shrugged his shoulders, and replied. *"It's partly my fault son."*

"Look daddy, those soldiers are wearing a different uniform. What is that sign on their sleeve?"

Dad lowered his head and turned the other way.

"Daddy, daddy — "what are they shouting?"

Daddy reached down and patted his son on the head. *"If only I . . ."*

"What did you say daddy?"

"Son, I will explain all of this when we get home. Now, let's just enjoy the parade."

On the way home, Devin was full of questions.

"Did you enjoy the parade?" Devin asked.

"Somewhat," dad replied while stopping at the red light.

"Daddy, I didn't see any American flags . . . and no one in the crowd was waving a flag.

I told you son, "we will finish this when we get home. Now let me drive — no more questions," moisture forming in his eyes.

"I hope mommy has some beef stew and cornbread ready for us. How about you? Are you hungry?"

"I'm starved. But I do have more questions."

They unbuckled, slid out of the car and raced to the front door. Laughing, Devin looked up — "beat you again daddy."

The door swung open — both of them were greeted by the lady of the house. She kissed her husband and reaching down, kissed Devin on the head.

"Are my men ready to eat?" she asked.

"Absolutely," came the reply.

"Go and wash up while I get the bread out of the oven," she told them, walking to the bathroom.

Mom scooped up the stew, and placed it in a beautiful off white tureen. She set it on the dining room table, along with the sliced cornbread and glasses of milk.

They bowed their heads and gave thanks.

"Well, how was the parade. Anyone want to start?" asked Mom.

Devin spoke up, "it was ok. Not like it used to be mommy — with the American flags waving in the air."

"I know son. Things are different now than when your dad and I were growing up."

Daddy gulped for air, turned his head, and stared out the window.

"Michael, what's wrong?" she asked.

"Nothing honey?"

"What do you mean nothing honey? Something is brothering you and we need to talk."

"Devin asked me some hard questions at the parade and I don't really know where to start."

"Well, after I finish with the dishes, we are going to answer his questions — whatever they are," she said.

After the dishes were washed and put away, mom retired to the den — reached over and turned the television off.

"Why did you do that mom?" Devin asked.

"Something happened at the parade and we are going to get to the bottom of it — right now. Now, who wants to tell me what's going on?"

"Honey, it's all my fault," he said, tears ran down his face. "Not one time in all my years as a pastor, did I mention the evil in politics or how it influenced our society?"

She reached for his hands. Holding them tight she whispered, "you did what you thought was best."

"That's true. But no time did I address our congregation to stand up and be accountable. The church was silent when the atheist had prayer removed from the schools. Now, look where we are — on the brink of destruction, by giving in to the political correctness of Islam and Sharia."

"Honey, you weren't the only one. Other pastors didn't have the foresight to see what was coming down the road."

"God, forgive me."

"How can we explain this to our son?" he asked.

Daddy put his arm around Devin, pulling him close to his chest. "Devin, I love you with all of my heart. What I am going to tell you will effect you for the rest of your life. There may come a time, when you, your brother and sister can forgive me, clearing his throat. and my generation for not fighting the evil that came upon us."

"What do you mean daddy?

"I was so interested in taking care of the church, that I let other things slip under the radar. Remember you can't pray in school and in some schools you can't read the Bible or even say the Pledge of Allegiance."

"Yes daddy. I would try and pray at lunch time and the monitor scolded me, so I would just bow my head and speak silently to God."

"Due to our political system, the nation elected the first black president. He campaigned on "hope" and "change" and the people believed him."

"What does campaign mean? And then you said,

political system. I don't understand those terms."

"They are hard to understand, even for us adults. We want to believe our politicians, but it appears they are only power and control hungry. Let me explain it a way you can understand."

"Do you remember the "Power Rangers?" — the good guys. They are always fighting evil or bad guys and they always win."

"Does the "Power Rangers" work for our government?" Devin asked.

"Not really son."

What daddy is trying to say — we let the bad guys win. We failed to stand up and fight and being silent just allowed the bad guys to win," mommy said.

"I don't understand all of this. But if you say so."

At the breakfast table the next morning, after Devin had gone to school, Michael sat there contemplating what his choices were, while finishing the cup of coffee.

"Honey, life is too short to let the enemy win, and have Devin and the other children go through hell just because I was silent. Do you remember Karl at church mentioning about a organization called Act for America. Well, I'm calling Karl and see when the next chapter is meeting."

"Are you sure this is what you want to do? What will your deacon board say?"

"I'm sorry, but this is too important not only for us, but for the whole church family and all of America.

"I'll be in my office if you need me. I need to spend some time in prayer."

Opening the door to the office, a bright light illuminated the room, compelling Michael to fall to his knees and bow, tears began to flow.

"Oh God, Oh God!"

Three hours later —-

Michael, lifting himself from the floor staggered to his desk. Taking a seat in the black leather chair, he turned the chair and stared out the window. His mind drew a blank. Nothing moved him until he noticed a mother bird fly to her nest with morsels. He muttered, "thank you, Lord."

Gaining his composure, Michael penned a few words on the yellow note pad . . . . *"God wants me to feed my congregation with the truth of His word. If God can take care of the sparrows, he can take care of us."*

Opening the computer, he typed in the words Act for America. The site opened showing a message from the president and founder, Brigitte Gabriel. Ms. Gabriel, is a survivor of a 1978 Lebanese Civil War. Islamic Militants launched an assault on a military base, destroying her nearby home in the attack. Brigitte's family had to seek shelter elsewhere. For 7 years, the family lived in a bomb shelter and only left the shelter for necessities. When Israelis soldiers invaded Lebanon, it provided a way of escape from this horrible dungeon and nightmare. In a matter of months, circumstances allowed her to make the journey to Israel, and later immigrated to the United States.

When all hell broke loose on 9/11, she declared: **"they are here,"** referring to Islam and Muslim radicals. In the months that followed, she addressed the threat to whomsoever would give her an ear. When her message fell on deaf ears, she formed Act for America, with its mission and goal of providing American citizens with a means to be a collective voice for the democratic values of Western Civilization and against the threat of radical Islam. On the side of the home page, a list of books and videos that one could view or order. He viewed several video trailers and read excerpts of a book that discussed Sharia in America.

Turning from the computer, Michael picked up the pad, writing several questions that need an answer:

Why Are Pastors Cowering in the Pulpit?
Talking to himself, he wrote the answer:
Under the Constitution of the United States, any person has the right to freely practice their religion. How-

ever, no religion has the right to impose its values upon others. What is more outrageous is the fact that the vast majority of our pastors are sitting inside the four walls, while the abuse of people of the Christian faith is taking place.

"Ouch, that hurts," he bellowed, writing . . .

"Who am I. Am I any better than the disciples or others that paid the supreme price for being a Christian?" he mumbled.

Most of the disciples of Jesus Christ were martyred for their uncompromising views towards corrupt civil authority, except for John, who died of extreme old age. For example, Peter was crucified; head downward, during persecution under Nero. James, was thrown from a pinnacle of the Temple, and then beaten to death. Thomas, the doubter, was run through the body with a lance at Coromandel, in the East Indies. As mentioned, the others met a violent death.

Michael placed the pen on the desk . . . pondering the words he had just written.

A stinging question flowed from his heart.

"Are you any different than the disciples or even the 57 men that signed the Declaration of Independence?"

Pastors need to be *men of faith* with courage, not sniveling, greedy wimps, who are cowering in the pulpit while they watch their religion being obliterated.

Next, the words came alive.

Sharia is alive and well in America.

Michael was exposed to other critical matters, pertaining as it had to his son, Devin.

In the school's textbooks on history and social studies, he learned that the major portion — nearly 50 pages — are devoted to Islam and their prophet and only 5 pages devoted to the teachings of Christianity. Reading further, he noticed that the major portion of the funds — 80% were supplied by Saudi Arabia.

He closed the computer. Standing to his feet, he walked to the window. Looking at the blue sky, he closed his hand, made a fist and hit the wall several times.

Nancy ran through the house and knocked on the door. "Michael, are you alright? I'm coming in." Cracking the door, she saw her husband leaning against the wall.

"Honey, do you want to talk?" she asked.

"Not right now. I need to filter all this information, myself," he told her. "In time, I need to know how God wants me to implement what I have learned. If we don't stand up against this demonic evil, it will consume us all."

Sticks and Stones

may break my bones, but
words will never hurt me!

The fallacy of this statement is twofold. One, sticks and stones will certainly hurt and perhaps break your bones and two, words have a different meaning. A sharp tongue can create falsehoods, or as the scripture states, "a lying tongue" — then there's words of anger, malice, hate and words that destroy a relationship.

America is being deceived today due to a lack of knowledge and insight into the religion of Islam. As stated elsewhere in the novel, it is horrendous, and our preference for "tolerance" misleads the public about the truth of the militant faith.

At a street festival in Washington, D.C., the crowd swayed to the rap music but it was not the words of many top rap stars singing about cop-killing, killing your mother or degrading women in gentle, it is a call of praise to Allah.

As the mostly black crowd lingered around the singer — they began to chant the words: *M U S L I M.*
So always be proud, you can say it out loud.
I am proud to be down
With the Muslim crowd! M U S L I M

Ramadan is here
The blessed month of the year
Fasting and not eating food
Acting nice and not bein' rude
Instead of watching movies today
Let's go to the majlis to pray.

So always be proud, you can say it out loud.
I am proud to be down
With the Muslim crowd! M U S L I M

This, so much reminds me of the Pentecostal Church in the 50's and 60's, with *strict rules* about serving God with fervency, joy and consuming desire to serve.

These are devout Muslims, and their dream is to inspire young people to "turn on" to Allah.

Five times a day, nearly 1.5 billion people bow their knee to Allah. In most of the Christian world, the people were forced to convert or be killed — thus their growth is due to the sword — by killing the infidel or apostate. In America, Muslims do not dare to force conversion, but as their numbers increase to 8-10-12-14% of the population, they will demand more and more from the political arena — like Sharia Law, Muslim no-go zones and kill the infidel when possible.

With Saudi money, to the tune of 20-25 million, our universities have Middle East Studies, using their own Muslim professors while patriotic Americans, Christians and Jews are refused to debate or carry on a conversation.

The great spawning ground for Islam is our prison system. We now have Muslim chaplains and guards who push Islam and the word has been passed to the *"blacks,"* that when Islam comes to power in America, all black prisoners will be released.

No wonder there's so many conversion.

They can take their revenge on "whitey" and they can't be prosecuted. Blacks relish in this thought — get even.

When our President and his top leaders continually call many of the outrageous assaults on Americans as "work place violence," "random walk up" shooting in the LA Airport or the beheading by a Muslim in Oklahoma as "anger violence," or the Fort Hood slaughter of our soldiers, as again "workplace violence" — it feeds the beast that they can do whatsoever they like and be covered by this administration and progressives and many conservatives — afraid to say the words: "terrorist, Islamphobia, jihad" and other names that relate to Islam.

One family group controls nearly 500 trillion dollars in assets, enough along with other wealthy members of the *Ring of Ten* to control the currency of nearly every nation on earth.

In his book, *Confessions of an Economic Hit Man*, the author, John Perkins explained how it works. The bankers use their control of currency to impose debt slavery on individuals as well as nations. They force nations to accept loans (America owes these bankers over 18 trillion plus dollars and counting) that are impossible to pay back—by design. The bankers use the resulting bankruptcy and/or 'restructuring agreements' to seize control of those nations and their resources.

What happens if a president or leader doesn't play ball or refuses to obey the bankers, (as is the case Iran and Venezuela — that leader, or nation, is put on the bankers "hit list. "

What is a "hit list?"

This hit list includes regime change by assassination, coup d'état, a bought or stolen election or outright invasion.

The bankers use the military and intelligence services of the nations they control to attack and subvert the nations they do not control. They also, have under their private control, armies which offer services or intelligence services to subvert all nations.

These international banking families exert a relatively high degree of control over the United States, Israel, Qatar, Turkey, Saudi Arabia and other nations. Thus, it is a banker's war in the Middle East, pushing for regime change in Syria — again total control as they gain country after country with the debt slave position.

The Federal Reserve:

In 1913, President Woodrow Wilson, needing finances to promote his presidency campaign, surrendered to the Ring of Ten and approved the Federal Reserve Act after he became president of the United States.

A few years later, he reflected — *"I am a most unhappy man. I have unwittingly ruined my country. A great industrial nation is controlled by its system of credit. Our system of credit is concentrated. The growth of the nation, therefore, and all our activities are in the hands of a few men (Ring of Ten). We have come to be one of the worst ruled, one of the most completely controlled and dominated governments in the civilized world — no longer a government by free opinion, no longer a government y conviction and the vote of the majority, but a government by the opinion and duress of a small group of dominant men. (Ring of Ten)*

David Rockefeller spoke the truth at the 1991 Bilderberg meeting in Baden, Germany: "We are grateful to the Washington Post, The New York Times, Time Magazine and other great publications whose directors have attended our meeting and respected their promises of discretion for almost 40 years.

It would have been impossible for us to develop our plan for the world if we had

been subjected to the lights of publicity
during those years. But, the world is now
more sophisticated and prepared to march
towards a world government. The supra-
national sovereignty of an intellectual
elite and world bankers is surely preferable
to the national auto-determination practiced
in past centuries."   end of quote

At the present time, they control all major media and newspaper companies. With this control, they are able to sensor any and all material that flows into your living room.

Not only the communication empire of America, they also control both major political parties — "the love of money is the root of all evil." Money is not evil. It is how money, power, control and prestige is used. Good or evil.

Our present president has been pushed to the forefront by the *Ring,* (who is this man in the White House) and is abiding by their script in deluding our Constitution with the mighty pen.

The bankers are not prejudice, they want (as do Islam) to make slaves of the entire world.

Side Bar:

Thomas Jefferson:

"If the American people ever allow private banks

to control the issue of their currency, first by inflation, then by deflation, the banks, will deprive the people of all property until their children wake up homeless on the continent their fathers conquered. The issuing power should be taken from the banks and restored to the people, to whom it properly belongs."

President John F. Kennedy:

President Kennedy was ready to sign an executive order nullifying President Wilson's Federal Reserve Act, which would have crimped the Ring of Ten's intentions of controlling not only America but other countries as well.

Is it possible this is why he was assassinated?

The Council on Foreign Relations (CFR) is another group that adheres to the end time doctrine of a New World Order.

In a Spotlight newspaper, dated October 22, 1990, they list many of the elite, including the Rockefeller family, major figures in the media, academia and the corporate, legal and financial worlds. There is also a significant number of government officials (both elected and appointed who serve as CFR members of this prestige New World Order.

The New World Order is nothing new, it is generations old, but it stuck its ugly head up when the premise of the League of Nations was conceived and later, the basis upon which the United Nations was established.

Only now, however, as a result of the crisis in the Middle East, have those who have been scheming for a new world order begun to talk publicly of the ultimate aim; one world government.

It has taken them until now to see their globalist dream placed within their reach.

As early as 1974, the Council on Foreign Relations launched its "1980 Project" which had its aim . . . "nothing less than the creation of a new global political and economic system to replace the existing one."

Today, the United Nations . . . CFR creation is playing a pivotal role in the Middle East . . . (with Obama subverting our Constitution in favor of the United Nations and International law) which allows the CFR to sell the American people a "bill of goods."

Spotlight News list some of the players . . . David Rockefellow, ex-president George H.W. Bush, Dan Quayle, James Baker, Richard Cheney, Colin Powell and other cabinet members in the Bush administration.

Alan Greenspan, Federal Reserve, JP Morgan-Chase Corp. Citicorp-Citibank, Bankers Trust of New York and First National Bank of Chicago — their CEO, Presidents and other officers.

Judiciary: Supreme Court Justice Ruth Ginsburg and Steven Breyer.

Media: CBS, NBC, ABC, Public Broadcast, Associated Press, Reuters, Washington Times, New York Times, Time Inc., Newsweek/Washington Post, Dow

Jones—Wall Street Journal and National Review.

Energy Companies: Exxon, Texaco, Shell Oil and Mobil Corp.

Industry: IBM, Amtrak, AT&T, Chrysler Corp., General Motors Corp., Ford Motor Co. and General Electric Co.

Universities: (a portion) Columbia, Cornell, New York, Stanford, Yale, John Hopkins, Princeton, Wisconsin, Texas, Brown and many more.

Note: *CFR/TC members head State Department bureaus where dramatic shifts in American foreign policy appear to work against allies of the United States and in favor of revolutionary forces.*

Sources: *1. The United States Government Manual 1989/90 Office of the Federal Register — National Archives and Records Administration, revised July 1, 1989. 2. Standard & Poor's Register of Corp, Director and Executives, 1989.*

Note: *The New World Order vision of Rockefeller and Kissinger and others in the CFR/TC "inner circle" are not shared by all members. Some join for prestige and to further their careers. However, Americans should be full informed of what the "Ring" is capable of doing in destroying America.*

Sometime in the future, a man will rise from the "Ring," be promoted through the United Nations, to rule the entire world.

The Bible calls this man the anti-christ. Satan will give him great power, wherewith he will reap havoc on the world in establishing the New World Order.

> *"And he causeth all, both small and great, rich*
> *and poor, free and enslaved, to receive a mark*
> *in their right hand or in their forehead."*
> *Revelation 13:16*

Those that receive this mark of the beast will be doomed. They will be judged at the "Great White Throne" judgment and those not found written in the Lamb's Book of Life will be cast into hell with Satan and all his demonic angels and demons to live forever and ever in the flames of hell.

> *"For God so loved the world that he gave*
> *His only Begotten Son, that whosoever*
> *believeth in Him should not perish but*
> *have ever lasting life.*
> *John 3:16*

A new World coming:

"And I John saw the holy City, New Jerusalem, coming down from God out of heaven, prepared as a Bride adorned for her Husband.

And I heard a great voice out of heaven saying, behold, the Tabernacle of God is with men, and he will dwell with them, and they shall be his people, and God himself shall be with them and be their God.

And God shall wipe away all tears from their eyes; and there shall be no more death, neither shall there be any more pain; for the former things are passed away.

And he that sat upon the throne said, Behold, I make all things new. And he said unto me, Write: for these words are true and faithful."

Revelation 21: 2-5

With the rise of the Russian Bear; the Chinese Dragon, ISIS and the restoration of the Caliphate in Turkey, "where does that leave the Eagle of America?"

Are there still Christians in Western Civilization or are they extinct, murdered or was there a mysterious disappearance of the so called "church."

Derek, rises from the ashes . . . leading the United Nations . . . setting up a New World Order.

Tick-Tock, the sequel to Ring of Fire

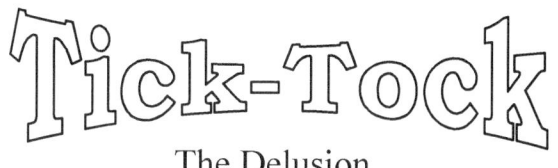

Tick-Tock
The Delusion
World War III or the End of the Game

Apocalypse

Hollywood is basking in the limelight of producing END OF THE WORLD movies as we know it.

The outlook for humanity seems a tad bleak.

We've been fighting *Cannibalistic Zombies* that have destroyed civilizations on *"The Walking Dead"* and aliens that have destroyed civilization in *"Falling Skies."* The Nanbots that destroyed civilization by eating electricity on *"Revolution"*. Then there's *"The Helix,"* a virus that destroys civilization and according to *"The 100,"* we are just a few years away from a nuclear war.

Now we have *"The Last Ship"* or even the virus that turns people into 'vampires, threatening the world with destruction in the *"The Strain,"* or *"The Giver"* movie.

Is *"Ebola"* the next strain that will wipe out or kill the majority of our population?

Dare Hollywood make a film about *Islam and Iran's nuclear weapons* wiping out Israel and or exploding a nuclear bomb in space causing an Electronic Magnetic Pulse that will literally fry our electrical grid—sending us back into time, the 1700's.

What Hollywood or TV producers fail to understand, is the Bible foretells an event, that will shake the very foundation of the universe—so BIG and VAST that millions upon millions will be slaughtered and the blood will flow so high, wide and deep — as described by John the Revelator — *"up to the bridle of a horse."*

The clock is ticking as scientist push the minute hand closer and closer to midnight when the final sound of the clock goes **tick-tock**, and what we now know as Mother Earth reeks with earthquakes, pestilences, darkness and the moon turning to blood.

>>>>

The Big Question:
Where is the church during all of this havoc?

What is meant by apostasy, deception and delusion?

Will the man — the anti-christ stand up?

If you enjoyed this novel, please comment or submit a review.

Ring of Fire

Revolution
The Battle for America's
Freedom and Liberty
Nicholas Fallon & R. L. Longworth

America at the crossroads. Will she survive? The Ring of Fire Brigade, has taken the charge to combat the liberal progressive agenda, in salvaging what is left of our beloved Republic. A revolution in the making.

Wallace Lane

A Nicholas Fallon Thriller

Intrigue, suspense, murder, spiritualism, and romance flows through the pages of Wallace Lane. Newspaper reporter Nicholas Fallon investigates the mysterious deaths of several people, missing over the years in cold cases coming alive.

Summer Love

A torrid summer affair on the beaches at Myrtle Beach, South Carolina, ends up at a home in Ashville, North Carolina.
A new arrival brings emotions, passion and stillness to the McKinley family — in Summer Love.

The Scorpion

Kelly Alexander,
US Marshal

A new adventure for one of the Alexander families favorite...US Marshal, the 3rd in this series.

Kentucky Homecoming

The year 1956....
A love story between two teens during their senior year. Nikki Jo is pregnant and Ryan is run out of town. He comes back for his mother's funeral and to settle her estate.
Will he rekindle his first love and will Nikki Jo respond, and there's little Emily, his daughter.

Facebook Assassin

RUSE—using Facebook and the internet to commit murder. A fired policeman and a geek (computer whiz) use the internet to target their victims in this thriller of real life.
Follow the trial leading to their arrest and death.

www.ingramcontent.com/pod-product-compliance
Lightning Source LLC
Chambersburg PA
CBHW071328280526
45787CB00001B/36